Non-League Football Supporters' Guide & Yearbook 2014

EDITOR
John Robinson

Twenty-second Edition

For details of our range of 2,000 books and over 400 DVDs, visit our web site or contact us using the information shown below.

British Library Cataloguing in Publication Data
A catalogue record for this book is available from the British Library

ISBN: 978-1-86223-269-3

Copyright © 2013, SOCCER BOOKS LIMITED (01472 696226)
72 St. Peter's Avenue, Cleethorpes, N.E. Lincolnshire, DN35 8HU, England

Web site www.soccer-books.co.uk • e-mail info@soccer-books.co.uk

Manufactured in the UK by Ashford Colour Press Ltd.

FOREWORD

Our thanks go to the numerous club officials who have aided us in the compilation of information contained in this guide as well as Michael Robinson (page layouts), Bob Budd (cover artwork) and Tony Brown (Cup Statistics – www.soccerdata.com).

Any readers who have up-to-date ground photographs which they would like us to consider for use in a future edition of this guide are requested to contact us at our address which is shown on the facing page.

The fixtures listed later in this book were released just a short time before we went to print and, as such, some of the dates shown may be subject to change. We therefore suggest that readers treat these fixtures as a rough guide and check dates carefully before attending matches.

Finally, we would like to wish our readers a safe and happy spectating season.

John Robinson
EDITOR

CONTENTS

THE FOOTBALL CONFERENCE NATIONAL

Address Third Floor, Wellington House, 31-34 Waterloo Street, Birmingham B2 5TJ

Phone (0121) 214-1950

Web site www.footballconference.co.uk

Clubs for the 2013/2014 Season

ALDERSHOT TOWN FC

Founded: 1992
Former Names: Aldershot FC
Nickname: 'Shots'
Ground: EBB Stadium, Recreation Ground, High Street, Aldershot   GU11 1TW
Record Attendance: 7,500 (18th November 2000)
Pitch Size: 117 × 76 yards

Colours: Red shirts with Blue trim, Red shorts
Telephone Nº: (01252) 320211
Fax Number: (01252) 324347
Club Secretary: (01252) 320211– Graham Hortop
Ground Capacity: 7,100
Seating Capacity: 1,879
Web site: www.theshots.co.uk
E-mail: enquiries@theshots.co.uk

GENERAL INFORMATION

Supporters Club: c/o Club
Telephone Nº: (01252) 320211
Car Parking: Municipal Car Park is adjacent
Coach Parking: Contact the club for information
Nearest Railway Station: Aldershot (5 mins. walk)
Nearest Bus Station: Aldershot (5 minutes walk)
Club Shop: At the ground
Opening Times: Matchdays only
Telephone Nº: (01252) 320211

GROUND INFORMATION

Away Supporters' Entrances & Sections:
Accommodation in the East Bank Terrace, Bill Warren section (South Stand) – Redan Hill Turnstiles Nº 11 and 12.

ADMISSION INFO (2013/2014 PRICES)

Adult Standing: £17.00
Adult Seating: £19.00
Under-16s Standing: £5.00 (Under-6s admitted free)
Under-16s Seating: £7.00
Concessionary Standing: £13.00
Concessionary Seating: £15.00
Note: Military personnel are charged Concessionary prices
Programme Price: £3.00

DISABLED INFORMATION

Wheelchairs: Accommodated in the North Stand
Helpers: Admitted
Prices: £13.00 for the disabled, free of charge for helpers
Disabled Toilets: Available
Contact: (01252) 320211   (Bookings are helpful)

Travelling Supporters' Information:
Routes: From the M3: Exit at Junction 4 and follow signs for Aldershot (A331). Leave the A331 at the A323 exit (Ash Road) and continue along into the High Street. The ground is just past the Railway Bridge on the right; From the A31: Continue along the A31 to the junction with the A331, then as above; From the A325 (Farnborough Road): Follow signs to the A323 then turn left into Wellington Avenue. The ground is just off the 2nd roundabout on the left – the floodlights are clearly visible.

ALFRETON TOWN FC

Founded: 1959
Former Names: None
Nickname: 'Reds'
Ground: The Impact Arena, North Street, Alfreton, Derbyshire   DE55 7FZ
Record Attendance: 5,023 vs Matlock Town (1960)
Pitch Size: 110 × 75 yards

Colours: Red shirts and shorts
Telephone Nº: (0115) 939-2090
Fax Number: (0115) 949-1846
Ground Capacity: 5,100
Seating Capacity: 1,600
Web site: www.alfretontownfc.com

GENERAL INFORMATION

Car Parking: At the ground
Coach Parking: Available close to the ground
Nearest Railway Station: Alfreton (½ mile)
Nearest Bus Station: Alfreton (5 minutes walk)
Club Shop: At the ground
Opening Times: Matchdays only
Telephone Nº: (01773) 830277

GROUND INFORMATION

Away Supporters' Entrances & Sections:
Segregation is usual so please check prior to the game

ADMISSION INFO (2013/2014 PRICES)

Adult Standing: £18.00
Adult Seating: £18.00
Senior Citizen Standing: £12.00
Senior Citizen Seating: £12.00
Under-16s Standing: £3.00 (with a paying adult)
Under-16s Seating: £3.00 (with a paying adult)

DISABLED INFORMATION

Wheelchairs: Accommodated in dedicated areas of the ground
Helpers: Admitted
Prices: Please phone the club for information
Disabled Toilets: Available
Contact: (01773) 830277   (Bookings are not necessary)

Travelling Supporters' Information:
Routes: Exit the M1 at Junction 28 and take the A38 signposted for Derby. After 2 miles take the sliproad onto the B600 then go right at the main road towards the town centre. After ½ mile turn left down North Street and the ground is on the right after 200 yards.

BARNET FC

No photograph of the new ground
was available at the time of going to print.

Founded: 1888
Former Names: Barnet Alston FC
Nickname: 'The Bees'
Ground: The Hive, Camrose Avenue, Edgware, HA8 6AG
Record Attendance: –
Pitch Size: 112 × 73 yards

Colours: Shirts and shorts are Black with Amber Trim
Telephone Nº: (020) 8381-3800
Ticket Office: (020) 8381-3800
Fax Number: –
Ground Capacity: 5,176
Seating Capacity: 3,434
Web site: www.barnetfc.com
E-mail: info@barnetfc.com

GENERAL INFORMATION

Car Parking: 350 spaces available at the ground
Coach Parking: Available at the ground
Nearest Railway Station: Harrow & Wealdstone (2½ miles)
Nearest Tube Station: Canons Park (15 minutes walk)
Club Shop: At the ground
Opening Times: Monday to Friday 10.00am to 5.00pm and Saturday Matchdays from 11.00am to 5.00pm
Telephone Nº: (020) 8381-3800

GROUND INFORMATION

Away Supporters' Entrances & Sections:
North Terrace and North West corner

ADMISSION INFO (2013/2014 PRICES)

Adult Standing: £16.00
Adult Seating: £21.00 – £23.00
Concessionary Seating: £13.00 – £15.00
Junior Bees (Under-14s): £5.00   (Members only)
Happy 9s Club (Ages 9 and under): £2.00 (Members only)
Away Supporters: £16.00 Standing;   £21.00 Seating
Programme Price: £3.00

DISABLED INFORMATION

Wheelchairs: 43 covered spaces in total for Home and Away fans in the East and West Stands
Helpers: One helper admitted per wheelchair
Prices: £21.00 for each fan with a wheelchair
Disabled Toilets: Available
Contact: (020) 8381-3800   (Bookings are not necessary)

Travelling Supporters' Information:
Routes: Exit the M1 at Junction 4 and take the Edgware Way/Watford Bypass (A41). Take the 3rd exit at the roundabout onto the A410 then the first exit at the next roundabout along the A5 (Stonegrove), continuing for approximately 1½ miles. Turn right into Camrose Avenue and The Hive is approximately two-thirds of a mile along this road.

BRAINTREE TOWN FC

Founded: 1898
Former Names: Manor Works FC, Crittall Athletic FC, Braintree & Crittall Athletic FC and Braintree FC
Nickname: 'The Iron'
Ground: Amlin Stadium, Clockhouse Way, Braintree, Essex CM7 3RD
Record Attendance: 4,000 (May 1952)
Pitch Size: 111 × 78 yards
Ground Capacity: 4,222
Seating Capacity: 556

Colours: Orange shirts and socks with Blue shorts
Telephone Nº: (01376) 345617
Fax Number: (01376) 330976
Correspondence Address: Tom Woodley, 19A Bailey Bridge Road, Braintree CM7 5TT
Contact Telephone Nº: (01376) 326234
Web site: www.braintreetownfc.org.uk
E-mail: braintreetfc@aol.com

GENERAL INFORMATION
Car Parking: At the ground
Coach Parking: At the ground
Nearest Railway Station: Braintree (1 mile)
Nearest Bus Station: Braintree
Club Shop: At the ground
Opening Times: Matchdays only
Telephone Nº: (01376) 345617

GROUND INFORMATION
Away Supporters' Entrances & Sections:
Gates 7-8

ADMISSION INFO (2013/2014 PRICES)
Adult Standing: £14.00 – £16.00
Adult Seating: £15.00 – £17.00
Senior Citizen Standing: £10.00
Under-16s Standing: £5.00
Under-11s Standing: £3.00
Note: Prices vary depending on the category of the game

DISABLED INFORMATION
Wheelchairs: Accommodated – 6 spaces available in the Main Stand
Helpers: Admitted
Prices: Normal prices apply
Disabled Toilets: Available
Contact: (01376) 345617

Travelling Supporters' Information:
Routes: Exit the A120 Braintree Bypass at the McDonald's roundabout and follow Cressing Road northwards. The floodlights at the ground are visible on the left ½ mile into town. Turn left into Clockhouse Way then left again for the ground.

CAMBRIDGE UNITED FC

Founded: 1912
Former Name: Abbey United FC (1912-1951)
Nickname: 'U's' 'United'
Ground: The R Costings Abbey Stadium, Newmarket Road, Cambridge CB5 8LN
Ground Capacity: 8,339
Seating Capacity: 4,376
Pitch Size: 110 × 74 yards

Record Attendance: 14,000 (1st May 1970)
Colours: Amber shirts, Black shorts
Telephone Nº: (01223) 566500
Ticket Office: (01223) 566500
Fax Number: (01223) 729220
Web Site: www.cambridgeunited.com
E-mail: info@cambridge-united.co.uk

GENERAL INFORMATION

Car Parking: Street parking only
Coach Parking: Coldhams Road
Nearest Railway Station: Cambridge (2 miles)
Nearest Bus Station: Cambridge City Centre
Club Shop: At the ground
Opening Times: Monday to Friday 9.30am to 4.00pm and Matchdays 11.00am to kick-off
Telephone Nº: (01223) 566500

GROUND INFORMATION

Away Supporters' Entrances & Sections:
Coldham Common turnstiles 20-22 – Habbin Terrace (South) and South Stand (Seating) turnstiles 23-26

ADMISSION INFO (2013/2014 PRICES)

Adult Standing: £15.00
Adult Seating: £17.00 – £19.00
Under-16s Standing: £5.00
Under-16s Seating: £6.00 – £9.00
Junior U's Standing: £2.00
Junior U's Seating: £3.00
Concessionary Standing: £10.00
Concessionary Seating: £11.00 – £12.00

DISABLED INFORMATION

Wheelchairs: 19 spaces in total for Home fans in the disabled sections, in front of Main Stand and in the North Terrace. 16 spaces for Away fans in the South Stand.
Helpers: One helper admitted per disabled fan
Prices: £10.00 – £12.00 for the disabled. Free for helpers
Disabled Toilets: At the rear of the disabled section
Contact: (01223) 566500 (Early booking strongly advised)

Travelling Supporters' Information: From the North: Take the A14 from Huntingdon, then turn east along the A14 dual carriageway. Exit the A14 at the 4th junction (to the east of Cambridge), up the slip road signposted Stow-cum-Quy then turn right onto the A1303, returning westwards towards Cambridge. Go straight on at the first roundabout passing the Airport on the left then straight on at two sets of traffic lights. Go straight on at the next roundabout and the ground is on the left after 700 yards; From the South: Exit the M11 at Junction 14 and turn east along the A14 dual carriageway. Then as from the North.
Bus Services: Services from the Railway Station to the City Centre and Nº 3 from the City Centre to the Ground.

CHESTER FC

Founded: 1885
Former Names: Chester FC and Chester City FC
Nickname: 'City'
Ground: Exacta Stadium, Bumpers Lane, Chester, CH1 4LT **Ground Telephone Nº**: (01244) 371376
Pitch Size: 116 × 75 yards

Record Attendance: 5,987 (17th April 2004)
Colours: Blue and White striped shirts, Black shorts
Ticket Office: (01244) 371376
Fax Number: (01244) 390265
Ground Capacity: 5,556 **Seating Capacity**: 4,170
Web site: www.chesterfc.com

GENERAL INFORMATION

Car Parking: Ample spaces available at the ground (£1.00)
Coach Parking: Available at the ground
Nearest Railway Station: Chester (2 miles)
Nearest Bus Station: Chester (1½ miles)
Club Shop: At the ground
Opening Times: Weekdays & matchdays 10.00am–4.00pm
Telephone Nº: (01244) 371376

GROUND INFORMATION

Away Supporters' Entrances & Sections:
South Stand for covered seating and also part of the West Stand

ADMISSION INFO (2013/2014 PRICES)

Adult Standing: £14.00
Adult Seating: £16.00
Senior Citizen Standing: £10.00
Senior Citizen Seating: £11.00
Under-18s Seating/Standing: £6.00
Under-16s Seating/Standing: £3.00 (Under-5s free)

DISABLED INFORMATION

Wheelchairs: 32 spaces for wheelchairs (with 40 helpers) in the West Stand and East Stand
Helpers: One helper admitted per disabled person
Prices: Concessionary prices for the disabled. Free for helpers
Disabled Toilets: Available in West and East Stands
Contact: (01244) 371376 (Bookings are necessary)

Travelling Supporters' Information:
Routes: From the North: Take the M56, A41 or A56 into the Town Centre and then follow Queensferry (A548) signs into Sealand Road. Turn left at the traffic lights by 'Tesco' into Bumpers Lane – the ground is ½ mile at the end of the road; From the East: Take the A54 or A51 into the Town Centre (then as North); From the South: Take the A41 or A483 into Town Centre (then as North); From the West: Take the A55, A494 or A548 and follow Queensferry signs towards Birkenhead (A494) and after 1¼ miles bear left onto the A548 (then as North); From the M6/M56 (Avoiding Town Centre): Take the M56 to Junction 16 (signposted Queensferry), turn left at the roundabout onto A5117, signposted Wales. At the next roundabout turn left onto the A5480 (signposted Chester) and after approximately 3 miles take the 3rd exit from the roundabout (signposted Sealand Road Industrial Parks). Go straight across 2 sets of traffic lights into Bumpers Lane. The ground is ½ mile on the right.

DARTFORD FC

Founded: 1888
Former Names: None
Nickname: 'The Darts'
Ground: Princes Park Stadium, Grassbanks, Darenth Road, Dartford   DA1 1RT
Record Attendance: 4,097 (11th November 2006)
Pitch Size: 110 × 71 yards

Colours: White Shirts with Black Shorts
Telephone Nº: (01322) 299990
Fax Number: (01322) 299996
Ground Capacity: 4,097
Seating Capacity: 640
Web Site: www.dartfordfc.co.uk
E-mail: info@dartfordfc.co.uk

GENERAL INFORMATION

Car Parking: At the ground
Coach Parking: At the ground
Nearest Railway Station: Dartford (½ mile)
Nearest Bus Station: Dartford (½ mile) & Bluewater (2 miles)
Club Shop: At the ground
Opening Times: Matchdays only – 1.00pm to 6.00pm.
Telephone Nº: (01322) 299990

ADMISSION INFO (2013/2014 PRICES)

Adult Standing: £15.00
Adult Seating: £15.00
Senior Citizen/Concessionary Standing: £8.00
Senior Citizen/Concessionary Seating: £8.00
Under-12s Standing: £3.00
Under-12s Seating: £3.00

DISABLED INFORMATION

Wheelchairs: Accommodated
Helpers: Admitted
Prices: Concessionary prices for the disabled and helpers
Disabled Toilets: Available
Contact: (01322) 299991   (Bookings are not necessary)

Travelling Supporters' Information:
Routes: From M25 Clockwise: Exit the M25 at Junction 1B. At the roundabout, take the 3rd exit onto Princes Road (A225) then the second exit at the next roundabout. * Continue downhill to the traffic lights (with the ground on the left), turn left into Darenth Road then take the 2nd left for the Car Park; From M25 Anti-clockwise: Exit the M25 at Junction 2 and follow the A225 to the roundabout. Take the first exit at this roundabout then the 2nd exit at the next roundabout. Then as from * above.

FC HALIFAX TOWN

Founded: 1911 (Re-formed 2008)
Former Names: Halifax Town FC
Nickname: 'The Shaymen'
Ground: The Shay Stadium, Shay Syke, Halifax, HX1 2YT
Ground Capacity: 10,568
Seating Capacity: 5,285

Record Attendance: 4,023 (1st January 2011)
Pitch Size: 112 × 73 yards
Colours: Blue shirts and shorts
Telephone Nº: (01422) 341222
Fax Number: (01422) 349487
Web Site: www.halifaxafc.co.uk
E-mail: secretary@halifaxafc.co.uk

GENERAL INFORMATION

Car Parking: Adjacent to the East Stand and also Shaw Hill Car Park (Nearby)
Coach Parking: By arrangement with the Club Secretary
Nearest Railway Station: Halifax (10 minutes walk)
Nearest Bus Station: Halifax (15 minutes walk)
Club Shop: At the ground in the East Stand
Opening Times: Please phone for details
Telephone Nº: (01422) 341222 (to change during the 2011/12 season)

GROUND INFORMATION

Away Supporters' Entrances & Sections:
Skircoat Stand (Seating only)

ADMISSION INFO (2013/2014 PRICES)

Adult Standing/Seating: £17.00
Under-16s Standing/Seating: £8.00
Senior Citizen Standing/Seating: £13.00
Under-12s Standing/Seating: £6.00
Under-7s Standing/Seating: £3.00

DISABLED INFORMATION

Wheelchairs: 33 spaces available in total in disabled sections in the East Stand and South Stand
Helpers: One admitted free with each paying disabled fan
Prices: Free of charge for the disabled and helpers
Disabled Toilets: Available in the East and South Stands
Contact: (01422) 434212 (Bookings are not necessary)

Travelling Supporters' Information:
Routes: From the North: Take the A629 to Halifax Town Centre. Take the 2nd exit at the roundabout into Broad Street and follow signs for Huddersfield (A629) into Skircoat Road; From the South, East and West: Exit the M62 at Junction 24 and follow Halifax (A629) signs for the Town Centre into Skircoat Road then Shaw Hill for ground.

FOREST GREEN ROVERS FC

Founded: 1889
Former Names: Stroud FC
Nickname: 'The Rovers'
Ground: The New Lawn, Smiths Way,
Forest Green, Nailsworth, Gloucestershire, GL6 0FG
Record Attendance: 4,836 (3rd January 2009)
Pitch Size: 110 × 70 yards

Colours: Black and White striped shirts, Black shorts
Telephone Nº: (01453) 834860
Fax Number: (01453) 835291
Ground Capacity: 5,147
Seating Capacity: 2,500
Web site: www.forestgreenroversfc.com
E-mail: reception@forestgreenroversfc.com

GENERAL INFORMATION
Car Parking: At the ground
Coach Parking: At the ground
Nearest Railway Station: Stroud (4 miles)
Nearest Bus Station: Nailsworth
Club Shop: At the ground
Opening Times: Matchdays only
Telephone Nº: (01453) 834860

GROUND INFORMATION
Away Supporters' Entrances & Sections:
EESI Stand

ADMISSION INFO (2013/2014 PRICES)
Adult Standing: £14.00   **Adult Seating**: £16.00
Senior Citizen Standing: £10.00
Senior Citizen Seating: £12.00
Child Standing: £4.00   **Child Seating**: £5.00
Young Adult Standing: £7.00
Young Adult Seating: £5.00

DISABLED INFORMATION
Wheelchairs: Accommodated in the Main Stand
Helpers: Admitted
Prices: Normal prices for the disabled. Free for helpers
Disabled Toilets: Yes
Contact: (01453) 834860   (Enquiries necessary at least 72 hours in advance)

Travelling Supporters' Information:
Routes: The ground is located 4 miles south of Stroud on the A46 to Bath. Upon entering Nailsworth, turn into Spring Hill at the mini-roundabout and the ground is approximately ½ mile up the hill on the left.

GATESHEAD FC

Founded: 1930   (Reformed in 1977)
Former Names: Gateshead United FC
Nickname: 'Tynesiders'
Ground: International Stadium, Neilson Road, Gateshead   NE10 0EF
Record Attendance: 11,750 (1995)
Pitch Size: 110 × 70 yards

Colours: White shirts with Black shorts
Telephone Nº: (0191) 478-3883
Fax Number: (0191) 440-0404
Ground Capacity: 11,750
Seating Capacity: 11,750
Web site: www.gateshead-fc.com
E-mail: info@gateshead-fc.com

GENERAL INFORMATION

Car Parking: At the stadium
Coach Parking: At the stadium
Nearest Railway Station: Gateshead Stadium Metro (½ mile); Newcastle (British Rail) 1½ miles
Nearest Bus Station: Heworth Interchange (½ mile)
Club Shop: At the stadium
Opening Times: Matchdays only
Telephone Nº: (0191) 478-3883

GROUND INFORMATION

Away Supporters' Entrances & Sections:
Tyne & Wear County Stand North End or the East Stand

ADMISSION INFO (2013/2014 PRICES)

Adult Seating: £14.00
Senior Citizen/Concessionary Seating: £9.00
Under-16s Seating: £2.00

DISABLED INFORMATION

Wheelchairs: 5 spaces available each for home and away fans by the trackside – Level access with automatic doors
Helpers: Admitted
Prices: Normal prices for the disabled. Helpers are admitted free of charge.
Disabled Toilets: Available in the Reception Area and on the 1st floor concourse – accessible by lift.
Contact: (0191) 478-3883   (Bookings are necessary)

Travelling Supporters' Information:
Routes: From the South: Take the A1(M) to Washington Services and fork right onto the A194(M) signposted Tyne Tunnel. At the next roundabout, turn left onto the A184 signposted for Gateshead. The Stadium is on the right after 3 miles.

GRIMSBY TOWN FC

Founded: 1878
Former Names: Grimsby Pelham FC (1879)
Nickname: 'Mariners'
Ground: Blundell Park, Cleethorpes   DN35 7PY
Ground Capacity: 8,974 (All seats)
Record Attendance: 31,651 (20th February 1937)
Pitch Size: 111 × 74 yards

Colours: Black and White striped shirts, Black shorts
Telephone Nº: (01472) 605050
Ticket Office: (01472) 605050
Fax Number: (01472) 693665
Web Site: www.grimsby-townfc.co.uk
E-mail: info@gtfc.co.uk

GENERAL INFORMATION

Car Parking: Street parking
Coach Parking: Harrington Street – near the ground
Nearest Railway Station: Cleethorpes (1½ miles)
Nearest Bus Station: Brighowgate, Grimsby (4 miles)
Club Shop: At the ground
Opening Times: Monday – Friday 9.00am to 5.00pm; Matchday Saturdays 9.00am to kick-off
Telephone Nº: (01472) 605050

GROUND INFORMATION

Away Supporters' Entrances & Sections:
Harrington Street turnstiles 15-18 and Constitution Avenue turnstiles 5-14

ADMISSION INFO (2013/2014 PRICES)

Adult Seating: £18.00 (Away fans £18.00)
Senior Citizen/Student Seating: £12.00
Young Adults Seating (Ages 15–18): £12.00
Child Seating: £4.00 – £6.00 (Under-15s)
Note: Tickets are cheaper if purchased before the matchday

DISABLED INFORMATION

Wheelchairs: 50 spaces in total for Home and Away fans in the disabled section, in front of the Main Stand
Helpers: Helpers are admitted
Prices: £18.00 for the disabled. Free of charge for helpers
Disabled Toilets: Available in disabled section
Commentaries are available in disabled section
Contact: (01472) 605050   (Bookings are necessary)

Travelling Supporters' Information:
Routes: From All Parts except Lincolnshire and East Anglia: Take the M180 to the A180 and follow signs for Grimsby/Cleethorpes. The A180 ends at a roundabout (the 3rd in short distance after crossing docks), take the 2nd exit from the roundabout over the Railway flyover into Cleethorpes Road (A1098) and continue into Grimsby Road. After the second stretch of dual carriageway, the ground is ½ mile on the left; From Lincolnshire: Take the A46 or A16 and follow Cleethorpes signs along (A1098) Weelsby Road for 2 miles. Take the 1st exit at the roundabout at the end of Clee Road into Grimsby Road. The ground is 1¾ miles on the right.

HEREFORD UNITED FC

Founded: 1924
Former Names: None
Nickname: 'United' 'The Bulls'
Ground: Edgar Street, Hereford   HR4 9JU
Record Attendance: 18,114 (4th January 1958)
Pitch Size: 110 × 70 yards

Colours: White shirts with Black shorts
Telephone Nº: 0844 276-1939
Fax Number: 0844 276-1982
Ground Capacity: 5,710
Seating Capacity: 3,390
Web site: www.herefordunited.co.uk
E-mail: club@herefordunited.co.uk

GENERAL INFORMATION
Car Parking: Merton Meadow Car Park (Near the ground)
Coach Parking: Merton Meadow Car Park
Nearest Railway Station: Hereford (½ mile)
Nearest Bus Station: Commercial Road, Hereford
Club Shop: At the ground
Opening Times: Weekdays 9.00am to 4.00pm and
Matchdays 12.00pm to 3.00pm
Telephone Nº: 0844 276-1939

GROUND INFORMATION
Away Supporters' Entrances & Sections:
Edgar Street entrances for the Edgar Street Stand and Terrace

ADMISSION INFO (2013/2014 PRICES)
Adult Standing: £12.00
Adult Seating: £17.00
Under-15s Standing: £3.00
Under-15s Seating: £5.00
Concessionary Standing: £10.00
Concessionary Seating: £14.00

DISABLED INFORMATION
Wheelchairs: 7 spaces in total for Home and Away fans in
the disabled section, Central Roofing Stand
Helpers: One helper admitted per disabled person
Prices: £12.00 for the disabled. Free of charge for helpers
Disabled Toilets: Available
Contact: 0844 276-1939   (Bookings are necessary)

Travelling Supporters' Information:
Routes: From the North: Follow A49 Hereford signs straight into Edgar Street; From the East: Take the A465 or A438 into
Hereford Town Centre, then follow signs for Leominster (A49) into Edgar Street; From the South: Take the A49 or A45 into the
Town Centre (then as East); From the West: Take the A438 into the Town Centre (then as East).

HYDE FC

Founded: 1885
Former Names: Hyde FC (1885-1917) and Hyde United FC (1917-2010)
Nickname: 'Tigers'
Ground: Ewen Fields, Walker Lane, Hyde, Cheshire, SK14 5PL
Record Attendance: 7,600 (vs Nelson, 1952)
Pitch Size: 114 × 70 yards

Colours: Red shirts with Navy Blue shorts
Telephone Nº: (0161) 367-7273
Fax Number: (0161) 367-7273
Ground Capacity: 4,073
Seating Capacity: 530
Web site: www.hydefc.co.uk
E-mail: secretary@hydefc.co.uk

GENERAL INFORMATION

Car Parking: 150 spaces available at the ground
Coach Parking: At the ground
Nearest Railway Station: Newton (¼ mile)
Nearest Bus Station: Hyde
Club Shop: At the ground
Opening Times: Matchdays only
Telephone Nº: (0161) 367-7273

GROUND INFORMATION

Away Supporters' Entrances & Sections:
No usual segregation although it is used as required. When segregation is in operation, Away supporter enter the turnstiles behind the Social Club or in the Walker Stand, as directed.

ADMISSION INFO (2013/2014 PRICES)

Adult Standing: £14.00
Adult Seating: £16.00
Child Standing: £4.00
Child Seating: £6.00
Senior Citizen Standing: £7.00
Senior Citizen Seating: £9.00

DISABLED INFORMATION

Wheelchairs: Accommodated in the disabled area
Helpers: Please phone the club for further information
Prices: Please phone the club for further information
Disabled Toilets: Yes
Contact: (0161) 367-7273   (Bookings are not necessary)

Travelling Supporters' Information:
Routes: Exit the M60 at Junction 24 and then exit the M67 at Junction 3 for Hyde. Turn right at the top of the slip road, left at the lights (Morrisons on the left). Turn right at the next set of lights into Lumn Road then turn left at the Give Way sign into Walker Lane. Take the 2nd Car Park entrance near the Leisure Pool and follow the road round for the Stadium.

KIDDERMINSTER HARRIERS FC

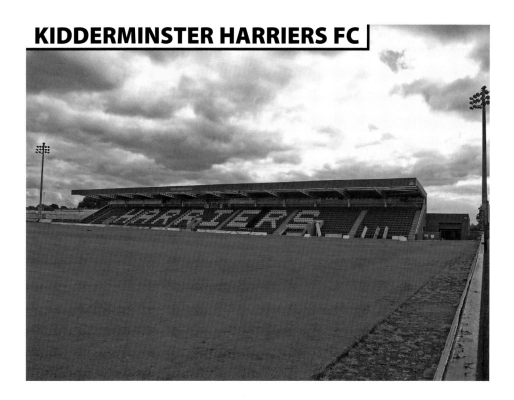

Founded: 1886
Nickname: 'Harriers'
Ground: Aggborough, Hoo Road, Kidderminster, Worcestershire DY10 1NB
Ground Capacity: 6,444
Seating Capacity: 3,143
Record Attendance: 9,155 (1948)

Pitch Size: 110 × 72 yards
Colours: Red shirts and shorts
Telephone Nº: (01562) 823931
Fax Number: (01562) 827329
Web Site: www.harriers.co.uk
E-mail: info@harriers.co.uk

GENERAL INFORMATION

Car Parking: At the ground
Coach Parking: As directed
Nearest Railway Station: Kidderminster
Nearest Bus Station: Kidderminster Town Centre
Club Shop: At the ground
Opening Times: Weekdays and First Team Matchdays 9.00am to 5.00pm
Telephone Nº: (01562) 823931

GROUND INFORMATION

Away Supporters' Entrances & Sections:
John Smiths Stand Entrance D and South Terrace Entrance E

ADMISSION INFO (2013/2014 PRICES)

Adult Standing: £14.00
Adult Seating: £17.00
Senior Citizen Standing: £8.00
Senior Citizen Seating: £11.00
Under-16s Standing: £5.00
Under-16s Seating: £8.00
Note: Under-5s are admitted free with a paying adult

DISABLED INFORMATION

Wheelchairs: Home fans accommodated at the front of the Main Stand, Away fans in front of the John Smiths Stand
Helpers: Admitted
Prices: £10.00 for each disabled fan plus one helper
Disabled Toilets: Available by the disabled area
Contact: (01562) 823931 (Bookings are not necessary)

Travelling Supporters' Information:
Routes: Exit the M5 at Junction 3 and follow the A456 to Kidderminster. The ground is situated close by the Severn Valley Railway Station so follow the brown Steam Train signs and turn into Hoo Road about 200 yards downhill of the station. Follow the road along for ¼ mile and the ground is on the left.

LINCOLN CITY FC

Founded: 1884
Nickname: 'Red Imps'
Ground: Sincil Bank Stadium, Lincoln   LN5 8LD
Ground Capacity: 10,120 (All seats)
Record Attendance: 23,196 (15th November 1967)
Pitch Size: 110 × 72 yards

Colours: Red and White striped shirts, Black shorts
Telephone Nº: (01522) 880011
Ticket Office: (01522) 880011
Fax Number: (01522) 880020
Web Site: www.redimps.com
E-mail: lcfc@redimps.com

GENERAL INFORMATION

Car Parking: Stacey West Car Park (limited parking for £5.00 per car).
Coach Parking: Please contact the club for details.
Nearest Railway Station: Lincoln Central
Club Shop: At the ground
Opening Times: Weekdays 10.00am to 2.00pm and Saturday Matchdays 10.00am until kick-off and 30 minutes after the final whistle
Telephone Nº: (01522) 880011

GROUND INFORMATION

Away Supporters' Entrances & Sections:
Lincolnshire Co-operative Stand (seated) – Turnstiles 24 & 25

ADMISSION INFO (2013/2014 PRICES)

Adult Seating: £16.00 – £18.00
Child Seating: £7.00
Concessionary Seating: £11.00 – £13.00
Note: Prices vary depending on the category of the game and area of the ground and discounts are available for advance ticket purchases

DISABLED INFORMATION

Wheelchairs: Limited number of spaces available in the disabled section, adjacent to turnstile 23
Helpers: One helper admitted per disabled person
Prices: Applications for disabled passes must be made to the club. Wheelchair-bound disabled are charged concessionary prices. Helpers are admitted free if the disabled fan has a medium/high level disability allowance
Disabled Toilets: Adjacent to disabled area
Contact: (01522) 880011   (Bookings are necessary)

Travelling Supporters' Information:
Routes: From the East: Take the A46 or A158 into the City Centre following Newark (A46) signs into the High Street and take next left (Scorer Street and Cross Street) for the ground; From the North and West: Take the A15 or A57 into the City Centre, then as from the East; From the South: Take the A1 then A46 for the City Centre, then into the High Street, parking on the South Common or in the Stadium via South Park Avenue, turn down by the Fire Station.

LUTON TOWN FC

Founded: 1885
Former Names: The club was formed by the amalgamation of Wanderers FC and Excelsior FC
Nickname: 'Hatters'
Ground: Kenilworth Road Stadium, 1 Maple Road, Luton LU4 8AW
Ground Capacity: 10,226 (All seats)
Record Attendance: 30,069 (4th March 1959)

Pitch Size: 110 × 72 yards
Colours: Orange shirts with Blue shorts
Telephone Nº: (01582) 411622
Ticket Office: (01582) 416976
Fax Number: (01582) 405070
Web Site: www.lutontown.co.uk
E-mail: info@lutontown.co.uk

GENERAL INFORMATION

Car Parking: Street parking
Coach Parking: Luton Bus Station
Nearest Railway Station: Luton (1 mile)
Nearest Bus Station: Bute Street, Luton
Club Shop: Kenilworth Road Forecourt
Opening Times: 10.00am to 5.00pm
Telephone Nº: (01582) 411622

GROUND INFORMATION

Away Supporters' Entrances & Sections:
Oak Road for the Oak Stand

ADMISSION INFO (2013/2014 PRICES)

Adult Seating: £15.00 – £18.00
Under-10s Seating: £5.00
Under-17s Seating: £8.00
Under-22s Seating: £13.00
Senior Citizen Seating: £10.00 – £13.00

DISABLED INFORMATION

Wheelchairs: 32 spaces in total for Home and Away fans in the disabled section, Kenilworth Road End and Main Stand
Helpers: One helper admitted per disabled person
Prices: £15.00 for the disabled. Free of charge for helpers
Disabled Toilets: Available adjacent to disabled area
Commentaries are available for the blind
Contact: (01582) 416976 (Bookings are necessary)

Travelling Supporters' Information:
Routes: From the North and West: Exit the M1 at Junction 11 and follow signs for Luton (A505) into Dunstable Road. Follow the one-way system and turn right back towards Dunstable, take the second left into Ash Road for the ground; From the South and East: Exit the M1 at Junction 10 (or A6/A612) into Luton Town Centre and follow signs into Dunstable Road. After the railway bridge, take the sixth turning on the left into Ash Road for the ground.

MACCLESFIELD TOWN FC

Founded: 1874
Former Names: Macclesfield FC
Nickname: 'The Silkmen'
Ground: Moss Rose Ground, London Road, Macclesfield, Cheshire   SK11 7SP
Ground Capacity: 6,335
Seating Capacity: 2,599
Record Attendance: 10,041 (1948)

Pitch Size: 110 × 66 yards
Colours: Blue shirts, White shorts and Blue socks
Telephone Nº: (01625) 264686
Ticket Office: (01625) 264686
Fax Number: (01625) 264692
Web Site: www.mtfc.co.uk
E-mail: office@mtfc.co.uk

GENERAL INFORMATION

Car Parking: Ample parking available near the ground
Coach Parking: Near the ground
Nearest Railway Station: Macclesfield (1 mile)
Nearest Bus Station: Macclesfield
Club Shop: At the ground
Opening Times: Weekdays and matchdays 9.00am to 5.00pm
Telephone Nº: (01625) 264686

GROUND INFORMATION

Away Supporters' Entrances & Sections:
Silkman Terrace and the left side of the McAlpine Stand

ADMISSION INFO (2013/2014 PRICES)

Adult Standing: £14.00
Adult Seating: £18.00
Concessions Standing: £10.00
Concessions Seating: £14.00
Under-12s Standing: £3.00
Under-12s Seating: £3.00
Ages 12-15 Standing: £5.00
Ages 12-15 Seating: £5.00

DISABLED INFORMATION

Wheelchairs: 45 spaces in front of the Estate Road Stand
Helpers: One helper admitted per disabled fan
Prices: Concessionary prices for the disabled. Helpers are admitted free of charge
Disabled Toilets: 3 available
Contact: (01625) 264686   (Bookings are necessary)

Travelling Supporters' Information:
Routes: From the North: Exit the M6 at Junction 19 to Knutsford, follow the A537 to Macclesfield. Follow signs for the Town Centre, then for the A523 to Leek. The ground is 1 mile out of the Town Centre on the right; From the South: Exit M6 at Junction 17 for Sandbach and follow the A534 to Congleton. Then take the A536 to Macclesfield. After passing The Rising Sun on the left, ¼ mile further on turn right after the Texaco Garage (Moss Lane). Following this lane will bring you back to the ground.

NUNEATON TOWN FC

Founded: 1937 (Reformed 2008)
Former Names: Nuneaton Borough FC
Nickname: 'Boro'
Ground: Sperrin Brewery Stadium, Liberty Way,
Attleborough Fields Industrial Estate, Nuneaton,
CV11 6RR
Record Attendance: 3,111 (2nd May 2009)
Pitch Size: 109 × 74 yards

Colours: Blue shirts and white shorts
Telephone Nº: (024) 7638-5738
Fax Number: (024) 7637-2995
Ground Capacity: 4,500
Seating Capacity: 500
Web site: www.nuneatontownfc.com
E-mail: admin@nuneatontownfc.com

GENERAL INFORMATION

Car Parking: On-site car park plus various other parking spaces available on the nearby Industrial Estate
Coach Parking: At the ground
Nearest Railway Station: Nuneaton (2 miles)
Nearest Bus Station: Nuneaton (2 miles)
Club Shop: Yes – The Boro Shop
Opening Times: By appointment and also on matchdays
Telephone Nº: (024) 7638-5738

GROUND INFORMATION

Away Supporters' Entrances & Sections:
No usual segregation

ADMISSION INFO (2012/2013 PRICES)

Adult Standing: £12.00
Adult Seating: £12.00
Concessionary Standing: £12.00
Concessionary Seating: £12.00
Under-16s Standing/Seating: £3.00
Note: Prices vary depending on the category of the game.

DISABLED INFORMATION

Wheelchairs: Accommodated
Helpers: Please phone the club for information
Prices: Please phone the club for information
Disabled Toilets: Available
Contact: (024) 7638-5738 (Bookings are necessary)

Travelling Supporters' Information:
Routes: From the South, West and North-West: Exit the M6 at Junction 3 and follow the A444 into Nuneaton. At the Coton Arches roundabout turn right into Avenue Road which is the A4254 signposted for Hinckley. Continue along the A4254 following the road into Garrett Street then Eastboro Way then turn left into Townsend Drive. Follow the road round before turning left into Liberty Way for the ground; From the North: Exit the M1 at Junction 21 and follow the M69. Exit the M69 at Junction 1 and take the 4th exit at the roundabout onto the A5 (Tamworth, Nuneaton). At Longshoot Junction, turn left onto the A47, continue to the roundabout and take the 1st exit onto A4254 Eastborough Way. Turn right at the next roundabout into Townsend Drive then immediately right again for Liberty Way.

SALISBURY CITY FC

Founded: 1947
Former Names: Salisbury FC
Nickname: 'The Whites'
Ground: The Raymond McEnhill Stadium, Partridge Way, Old Sarum, Salisbury, Wiltshire   SP4 6PU
Record Attendance: 3,408 (12th May 2013)
Pitch Size: 115 × 76 yards

Colours: Shirts and shorts are White with Black trim
Telephone Nº: (01722) 776655
Fax Number: (01722) 323100
Ground Capacity: 4,000
Seating Capacity: 606
Web site: www.salisburycity-fc.co.uk
E-mail: info@salisburycity-fc.co.uk

GENERAL INFORMATION

Car Parking: At the ground
Coach Parking: At the ground
Nearest Railway Station: Salisbury (3½ miles)
Nearest Bus Station: Salisbury
Club Shop: At the ground
Opening Times: Office Hours and Matchdays
Telephone Nº: (01722) 776655
Postal Sales: Yes

GROUND INFORMATION

Away Supporters' Entrances & Sections:
No usual segregation

ADMISSION INFO (2013/2014 PRICES)

Adult Standing: £14.00
Adult Seating: £16.00
Senior Citizen/Concessionary Standing: £12.00
Senior Citizen/Concessionary Seating: £14.00
Under-16s Standing: £5.00   (Free of charge for
Under-16s Seating: £7.00   ages 5 and under)
Student Standing: £10.00
Student Seating: £12.00

DISABLED INFORMATION

Wheelchairs: Accommodated in a special area in the Main Stand. A stairlift is available.
Helpers: Admitted free of charge
Prices: Normal prices apply for the disabled
Disabled Toilets: Available
Contact: (01722) 776655   (Bookings are necessary)

Travelling Supporters' Information:
Routes: The Stadium well signposted and is situated off the main A345 Salisbury to Amesbury road on the northern edge of the City, 2 miles from the City Centre.

SOUTHPORT FC

Founded: 1881
Former Names: Southport Vulcan FC, Southport Central FC
Nickname: 'The Sandgrounders'
Ground: Haig Avenue, Southport, Merseyside, PR8 6JZ
Record Attendance: 20,010 (1932)
Pitch Size: 110 × 77 yards

Colours: Yellow shirts and shorts
Telephone N°: (01704) 533422
Fax Number: (01704) 533455
Ground Capacity: 6,008
Seating Capacity: 1,660
Web site: www.southportfc.net

GENERAL INFORMATION

Car Parking: Street parking
Coach Parking: Adjacent to the ground
Nearest Railway Station: Meols Cop (½ mile)
Nearest Bus Station: Southport Town Centre
Club Shop: At the ground
Opening Times: Matchdays from 1.30pm (from 6.30pm on evening matchdays)
Telephone N°: (01704) 533422

GROUND INFORMATION

Away Supporters' Entrances & Sections:
Blowick End entrances

ADMISSION INFO (2013/2014 PRICES)

Adult Standing: £13.50
Adult Seating: £15.00
Concessionary Standing: £10.00
Concessionary Seating: £11.00
Under-19s Standing/Seating: £5.00
Note: Children aged 11 and under are admitted free of charge when accompanied by a paying adult.

DISABLED INFORMATION

Wheelchairs: Accommodated in front of the Grandstand
Helpers: Admitted
Prices: Concessionary prices charged for the disabled. Helpers are admitted free of charge
Disabled Toilets: Available at the Blowick End of the Grandstand
Contact: (01704) 533422 (Bookings are not necessary)

Travelling Supporters' Information:
Routes: Exit the M58 at Junction 3 and take the A570 to Southport. At the major roundabout (McDonalds/Tesco) go straight on into Scarisbrick New Road, pass over the brook and turn right into Haig Avenue at the traffic lights. The ground is then on the right-hand side.

TAMWORTH FC

Founded: 1933
Former Names: None
Nickname: 'The Lambs'
Ground: The Lamb Ground, Kettlebrook, Tamworth, B77 1AA
Record Attendance: 4,920 (3rd April 1948)
Pitch Size: 110 × 73 yards

Colours: Red shirts with Black shorts
Telephone Nº: (01827) 65798
Fax Number: (01827) 62236
Ground Capacity: 4,118
Seating Capacity: 520
Web site: www.thelambs.co.uk

GENERAL INFORMATION

Car Parking: 200 spaces available at the ground – £2.00 per car, £5.00 for per minibus or £10.00 per coach
Coach Parking: At the ground
Nearest Railway Station: Tamworth (½ mile)
Nearest Bus Station: Tamworth (½ mile)
Club Shop: At the ground
Opening Times: Weekdays from 10.00am to 4.00pm and also on Matchdays
Telephone Nº: (01827) 65798 Option 3

GROUND INFORMATION

Away Supporters' Entrances & Sections:
Gates 1 and 2 for Terracing, Gate 2A for seating

ADMISSION INFO (2013/2014 PRICES)

Adult Standing: £12.00 – £14.00
Adult Seating: £14.00 – £16.00
Under-16s Standing: £3.00 – £4.00   (Under-6s free)
Under-16s Seating: £5.00 – £6.00
Under-6s Seating: £3.00 – £5.00
Senior Citizen Standing: £7.00 – £9.00
Senior Citizen Seating: £9.00 – £11.00
Note: Prices vary depending on the category of the game.

DISABLED INFORMATION

Wheelchairs: Accommodated
Helpers: Admitted
Prices: Normal prices apply for Wheelchair disabled. Helpers are charged concessionary rates
Disabled Toilets: Yes
Contact: (01827) 65798   (Bookings are advisable)

Travelling Supporters' Information:
Routes: Exit the M42 at Junction 10 and take the A5/A51 to the town centre following signs for Town Centre/Snowdome. The follow signs for Kettlebrook and the ground is in Kettlebrook Road, 50 yards from the traffic island by the Railway Viaduct and the Snowdome. The ground is signposted from all major roads.

WELLING UNITED FC

Founded: 1963
Former Names: None
Nickname: 'The Wings'
Ground: Park View Road Ground, Welling, Kent, DA16 1SY
Record Attendance: 4,020 (1989/90)
Pitch Size: 112 × 72 yards

Colours: Shirts are Red with White facings, Red shorts
Telephone Nº: (0208) 301-1196
Daytime Phone Nº: (0208) 301-1196
Fax Number: (0208) 301-5676
Ground Capacity: 4,000
Seating Capacity: 500
Web site: www.wellingunited.com

GENERAL INFORMATION

Car Parking: Street parking only
Coach Parking: Outside of the ground
Nearest Railway Station: Welling (¾ mile)
Nearest Bus Station: Bexleyheath
Club Shop: At the ground
Opening Times: Matchdays only
Telephone Nº: (0208) 301-1196

GROUND INFORMATION

Away Supporters' Entrances & Sections:
Accommodation in the Danson Park End

ADMISSION INFO (2013/2014 PRICES)

Adult Standing: £15.00
Adult Seating: £16.00
Concessionary Standing: £9.00 – £10.00
Concessionary Seating: £10.00 – £11.00
Under-12s Standing: Free with a paying adult
Under-12s Seating: £1.00 with a paying adult

DISABLED INFORMATION

Wheelchairs: Accommodated at the side of the Main Stand
Helpers: Admitted
Prices: £7.50 for the disabled. Helpers pay normal prices
Disabled Toilets: Yes
Contact: (0208) 301-1196 (Bookings are not necessary)

Travelling Supporters' Information:
Routes: Take the A2 (Rochester Way) from London, then the A221 Northwards (Danson Road) to Bexleyheath. At the end turn left towards Welling along Park View Road and the ground is on the left.

WOKING FC

Founded: 1889
Former Names: None
Nickname: 'Cardinals'
Ground: Kingfield Stadium, Kingfield, Woking, Surrey   GU22 9AA
Record Attendance: 6,000 (1997)
Pitch Size: 109 × 76 yards

Colours: Shirts are Red & White halves, Black shorts
Telephone N°: (01483) 772470
Daytime Phone N°: (01483) 772470
Fax Number: (01483) 888423
Ground Capacity: 6,161
Seating Capacity: 2,511
Web site: www.wokingfc.co.uk
E-mail: admin@wokingfc.co.uk

GENERAL INFORMATION

Car Parking: Limited parking at the ground
Coach Parking: At or opposite the ground
Nearest Railway Station: Woking (1 mile)
Nearest Bus Station: Woking
Club Shop: At the ground
Opening Times: Weekdays and Matchdays
Telephone N°: (01483) 772470

GROUND INFORMATION

Away Supporters' Entrances & Sections:
Kingfield Road entrance for the Tennis Club terrace

ADMISSION INFO (2013/2014 PRICES)

Adult Standing: £15.00
Adult Seating: £15.00
Under-16s/Student Standing: £3.00
Under-16s/Student Seating: £3.00
Senior Citizen Standing: £10.00
Senior Citizen Seating: £10.00

DISABLED INFORMATION

Wheelchairs: 8 spaces in the Leslie Gosden Stand and 8 spaces in front of the Family Stand
Helpers: Admitted
Prices: One wheelchair and helper for £10.00
Disabled Toilets: Yes – in the Leslie Gosden Stand and Family Stand area
Contact: (01483) 772470   (Bookings are necessary)

Travelling Supporters' Information:
Routes: Exit the M25 at Junction 10 and follow the A3 towards Guildford. Leave at the next junction onto the B2215 through Ripley and join the A247 to Woking. Alternatively, exit the M25 at Junction 11 and follow the A320 to Woking Town Centre. The ground is on the outskirts of Woking – follow signs on the A320 and A247.

WREXHAM FC

Founded: 1864
Nickname: 'Red Dragons'
Ground: Racecourse Ground, Mold Road, Wrexham, North Wales   LL11 2AH
Ground Capacity: 10,500 (all seats)
Record Attendance: 34,445 (26th January 1957)
Pitch Size: 111 × 71 yards

Colours: Red shirts with White shorts
Telephone Nº: (01978) 262129
Fax Number: (01978) 357821
Web Site: www.wrexhamafc.co.uk
E-mail: info@wrexhamfc.tv

GENERAL INFORMATION

Car Parking: Town car parks are nearby and also Glyndwr University (Mold End)
Coach Parking: By Police direction
Nearest Railway Station: Wrexham General (adjacent)
Nearest Bus Station: Wrexham (King Street)
Club Shop: At the ground in the Yale Stand
Opening Times: Monday to Saturday 9.00am to 5.00pm
Telephone Nº: (01978) 262129

GROUND INFORMATION

Away Supporters' Entrances & Sections:
Turnstiles 1-4 for the Yale Stand

ADMISSION INFO (2013/2014 PRICES)

Adult Seating: £15.00 – £19.00
Under-16s Seating: £5.00
Under-11s Seating: £1.00 (with a paying adult)
Concessionary Seating: £10.00 – £12.00
Over-80s Seating: £5.00
Note: Family tickets are also available

DISABLED INFORMATION

Wheelchairs: 35 spaces in the Mold Road Stand
Helpers: One helper admitted per wheelchair
Prices: Normal prices for the disabled. Free for helpers
Disabled Toilets: Available in the disabled section
Contact: (01978) 262129   (Bookings are preferred)

Travelling Supporters' Information:
Routes: From the North and West: Take the A483 and the Wrexham bypass to the junction with the A541. Branch left at the roundabout and follow Wrexham signs into Mold Road; From the East: Take the A525 or A534 into Wrexham then follow the A541 signs into Mold Road; From the South: Take the the M6, then the M54 and follow the A5 and A483 to the Wrexham bypass and the junction with the A541. Branch right at the roundabout and follow signs for the Town Centre.

The Football Conference North

Address

Third Floor, Wellington House,
31-34 Waterloo Street, Birmingham   B2 5TJ

Phone (0121) 214-1950

Web site www.footballconference.co.uk

Clubs for the 2013/2014 Season

AFC TELFORD UNITED

Founded: 2004
Former Names: Formed after Telford United FC went out of business. TUFC were previously known as Wellington Town FC
Nickname: 'The Bucks'
Ground: The New Bucks Head Stadium, Watling Street, Wellington, Telford TF1 2TU
Record Attendance: 13,000 (1935)

Pitch Size: 110 × 74 yards
Colours: White shirts with Black shorts
Telehone Nº: (01952) 640064
Fax Number: (01952) 640021
Ground Capacity: 5,780
Seating Capacity: 2,280
Web site: www.telfordutd.co.uk

GENERAL INFORMATION

Car Parking: At the ground
Coach Parking: At the ground
Nearest Railway Station: Wellington
Nearest Bus Station: Wellington
Club Shop: At the ground
Opening Times: Tuesdays and Thursdays 4.00pm to 6.00pm and Saturday Matchdays from 1.30pm
Telephone Nº: None

GROUND INFORMATION

Away Supporters' Entrances & Sections:
Frank Nagington Stand on the rare occasions when segregation is used

ADMISSION INFO (2013/2014 PRICES)

Adult Standing: £14.00
Adult Seating: £15.00
Under-14s Standing: £2.00 (with a paying adult)
Under-14s Seating: £2.00 (with a paying adult)
Under-18s Standing: £6.00
Under-18s Seating: £7.00
Senior Citizen Standing: £11.00
Senior Citizen Seating: £12.00

DISABLED INFORMATION

Wheelchairs: Accommodated at both ends of the ground
Helpers: Admitted
Prices: Normal prices apply
Disabled Toilets: Available
Contact: (01952) 640064   (Bookings are not necessary)

Travelling Supporters' Information:
Routes: Exit the M54 at Junction 6 and take the A518. Go straight on at the first roundabout, take the second exit at the next roundabout then turn left at the following roundabout. Follow the road round to the right then turn left into the car park.

ALTRINCHAM FC

Founded: 1891
Former Names: Broadheath FC
Nickname: 'The Robins'
Ground: Moss Lane, Altrincham   WA15 8AP
Record Attendance: 10,275 (February 1925)
Pitch Size: 110 × 72 yards
Web site: www.altrinchamfc.com

Colours: Red and White striped shirts, Black shorts
Telephone Nº: (0161) 928-1045
Daytime Phone Nº: (0161) 928-1045
Fax Number: (0161) 926-9934
Ground Capacity: 6,085
Seating Capacity: 1,154
E-mail: office@altrinchamfootballclub.co.uk

GENERAL INFORMATION

Car Parking: Limited street parking
Coach Parking: By Police Direction
Nearest Railway Station: Altrincham (15 minutes walk)
Nearest Bus Station: Altrincham
Club Shop: Inside the ground
Opening Times: Matchdays only. Opens one hour prior to the start of the game.
Telephone Nº: (0161) 928-1045

GROUND INFORMATION

Away Supporters' Entrances & Sections:
Hale End turnstiles and accommodation

ADMISSION INFO (2013/2014 PRICES)

Adult Standing: £13.00
Adult Seating: £15.00
Concessionary Standing: £8.00
Concessionary Seating: £9.00
Ages 12-16 years Standing/Seating: £5.00
Under-12s Standing/Seating: £2.00

DISABLED INFORMATION

Wheelchairs: 3 spaces are available each for home and away fans adjacent to the Away dugout
Helpers: Admitted
Prices: Free for the disabled. £13.00 for helpers
Disabled Toilets: Yes
Contact: (0161) 928-1045   (Bookings are necessary)

Travelling Supporters' Information:
Routes: Exit the M56 at either Junction 6 or 7 and follow the signs for Altrincham FC.

BARROW FC

Founded: 1901
Former Names: None
Nickname: 'Bluebirds'
Ground: Furness Building Society Stadium, Barrow-in-Furness, Cumbria   LA14 5UW
Record Attendance: 16,874 (1954)
Pitch Size: 110 × 75 yards

Colours: White shirts with Blue shorts
Telephone Nº: (01229) 823061
Fax Number: (01229) 823061
Ground Capacity: 4,057
Seating Capacity: 928
Web site: www.barrowafc.com
E-mail: office@barrowafc.com

GENERAL INFORMATION

Car Parking: Street Parking, Popular Side Car Park and Soccer Bar Car Park
Coach Parking: Adjacent to the ground
Nearest Railway Station: Barrow Central (½ mile)
Nearest Bus Station: ½ mile
Club Shop: At the ground
Opening Times: Monday to Friday 9.00am – 3.30pm and Saturdays 10.00am – 2.00pm
Telephone Nº: (01229) 823061

GROUND INFORMATION

Away Supporters' Entrances & Sections:
West Terrace (not covered)

ADMISSION INFO (2013/2014 PRICES)

Adult Standing: £13.00
Adult Seating: £14.00
Concessionary Standing: £10.00
Concessionary Seating: £11.00
Under-18s Standing/Seating: £5.00
Under-7s Standing/Seating: £1.00

DISABLED INFORMATION

Wheelchairs: 6 spaces available in the Disabled Area
Helpers: Admitted
Prices: Normal prices apply
Disabled Toilets: Available
Contact: (01229) 823061   (Bookings are not necessary)

Travelling Supporters' Information:
Routes: Exit the M6 at Junction 36 and take the A590 through Ulverston. Using the bypass, follow signs for Barrow. After approximately 5 miles, turn left into Wilkie Road and the ground is on the right.

BOSTON UNITED FC

Founded: 1933
Former Names: Boston Town FC & Boston Swifts FC
Nickname: 'The Pilgrims'
Ground: Jakeman's Stadium, York Street, Boston, PE21 6JN
Ground Capacity: 6,613 **Seating Capacity**: 2,000
Pitch Size: 112 × 72 yards

Record Attendance: 10,086 (1955)
Colours: Amber and Black shirts, Black shorts
Telephone Nº: (01205) 364406 (Office)
Matchday Info: (01205) 364406 or 07860 663299
Fax Number: (01205) 354063
Web Site: www.bufc.co.uk
E-mail: admin@bufc.co.uk

GENERAL INFORMATION

Car Parking: Permit holders only
Coach Parking: Available near to the ground
Nearest Railway Station: Boston (1 mile)
Nearest Bus Station: Boston Coach Station (¼ mile)
Club Shop: In the car park at the ground
Opening Times: Weekdays from 9.00am to 5.00pm and Saturday Matchdays from 11.00am to 5.00pm
Telephone Nº: (01205) 364406

GROUND INFORMATION

Away Supporters' Entrances & Sections:
York Street Entrances 3 & 4 (subject to a move to the Jakemans Stand if so advised by the police)

ADMISSION INFO (2013/2014 PRICES)

Adult Standing: £12.00
Adult Seating: £14.00
Child Standing: £4.00
Child Seating: £5.00
Senior Citizen Standing: £9.00
Senior Citizen Seating: £10.00

DISABLED INFORMATION

Wheelchairs: 7 spaces available for home fans, 4 spaces for away fans below the Main Stand at the Town End
Helpers: One helper admitted per disabled fan
Prices: £12.00 for the disabled. Free of charge for helpers
Disabled Toilets: Available in the Town End Terrace
Contact: (01205) 364406 (Bookings are necessary)

Travelling Supporters' Information:
From the North: Take the A17 from Sleaford, bear right after the railway crossing to the traffic lights over the bridge. Go forward through the traffic lights into York Street for the ground; From the South: Take the A16 from Spalding and turn right at the traffic lights over the bridge. Go forward through the next traffic lights into York Street for the ground.

BRACKLEY TOWN FC

Founded: 1890
Former Names: None
Nickname: 'Saints'
Ground: St. James Park, Churchill Way, Brackley, NN13 7EJ
Record Attendance: 2,604 (2012/13 season)

Colours: Red and White striped shirts with Red shorts
Telephone Nº: (01280) 704077
Ground Capacity: 3,500
Seating Capacity: 300
Web Site: www.brackleytownfc.com

GENERAL INFORMATION

Car Parking: At the ground (£2.00 charge per car)
Coach Parking: At the ground
Nearest Railway Station: King's Sutton (6¾ miles)
Club Shop: At the ground
Opening Times: Matchdays and by appointment only
Telephone Nº: (01280) 704077

GROUND INFORMATION

Away Supporters' Entrances & Sections:
No usual segregation

ADMISSION INFO (2013/2014 PRICES)

Adult Standing: £10.00
Adult Seating: £10.00
Senior Citizen/Student Standing: £5.00
Senior Citizen/Student Seating: £5.00
Under-16s Standing: £2.00
Under-16s Seating: £2.00

DISABLED INFORMATION

Wheelchairs: Accommodated
Helpers: Admitted
Prices: Normal prices apply for the disabled and helpers
Disabled Toilets: Available
Contact: (01280) 704077 (Stephen Toghill – bookings are necessary)

Travelling Supporters' Information:
Routes: From the West: Take the A422 to Brackley and take the first exit at the roundabout with the junction of the A43, heading north into Oxford Road.* Go straight on at the next roundabout and continue into Bridge Street before turning right into Churchill Way. The ground is located at the end of the road; From the South: Take the A43 northwards to Brackley. Take the second exit at the roundabout with the junction of the A422 and head into Oxford Road. Then as from * above; From the North-East: Take the A43 to Brackley. Upon reaching Brackley, take the 1st exit at the 1st roundabout, the 2nd exit at the next roundabout then the 3rd exit at the following roundabout into Oxford Road. Then as from * above.

BRADFORD PARK AVENUE FC

Founded: 1907 (Re-formed in 1988)	**Colours**: Green & White striped shirts, White shorts
Former Names: None	**Telephone N°**: (01274) 604578 (Ground)
Nickname: 'Avenue'	**Office Address**: Hugh House, Foundry Street,
Ground: Horsfall Stadium, Cemetery Road, Bradford,	Brighouse HD6 1LT
BD6 2NG	**Office Number**: (01484) 400007
Record Attendance: 2,100 (2003)	**Ground Capacity**: 3,000 **Seating Capacity**: 1,247
Pitch Size: 112 × 71 yards	**Web site**: www.bpafc.com

GENERAL INFORMATION

Car Parking: Street parking and some spaces at the ground
Coach Parking: At the ground
Nearest Railway Station: Bradford Interchange (3 miles)
Nearest Bus Station: Bradford Interchange (3 miles)
Club Shop: At the ground
Opening Times: Matchdays only
Telephone N°: –

GROUND INFORMATION

Away Supporters' Entrances & Sections:
Segregation only used when required

ADMISSION INFO (2013/2014 PRICES)

Adult Standing/Seating: £11.00
Senior Citizen Standing/Seating: £7.00
Student Standing/Seating: £6.00
Under-16s Standing/Seating: £2.00
Armed Forces Standing/Seating: £2.00 (warrant card must be shown)

DISABLED INFORMATION

Wheelchairs: Accommodated in front of the Stand
Helpers: Please phone the club for information
Prices: Please phone the club for information
Disabled Toilets: Available
Contact: –   (Bookings are not necessary)

Travelling Supporters' Information:
Routes: Exit the M62 at Junction 26 and take the M606 to its end. At the roundabout go along the A6036 (signposted Halifax) and pass Odsal Stadium on the left. At the roundabout by Odsal take the 3rd exit (still A6036 Halifax). After just under 1 mile, turn left at the King's Head pub into Cemetery Road. The ground is 150 yards on the left.

COLWYN BAY FC

Founded: 1885
Former Names: None
Nickname: 'Bay' 'Seagulls'
Ground: Llanelian Road, Old Colwyn, Colwyn Bay, LL29 8UN
Record Attendance: 2,400

Colours: Sky Blue shirts with Maroon shorts
Telephone Nº: (01492) 514680
Ground Capacity: 2,500
Seating Capacity: 500
Web site: www.colwynbayfc.co.uk

GENERAL INFORMATION

Car Parking: At the ground
Coach Parking: At the ground
Nearest Railway Station: Colwyn Bay (1 mile)
Nearest Bus Station: Colwyn Bay (Nº 23 stops at ground)
Club Shop: At the ground
Opening Times: Weekdays from 10.00am to 4.00pm
Telephone Nº: (01422) 514680

GROUND INFORMATION

Away Supporters' Entrances & Sections:
No usual segregation

ADMISSION INFO (2013/2014 PRICES)

Adult Standing/Seating: £10.00
Concessionary Standing/Seating: £6.00
Student Standing/Seating: £6.00
Under-16s Standing/Seating: £3.00

DISABLED INFORMATION

Wheelchairs: Accommodated in Covered Shelter
Helpers: Admitted
Prices: Normal prices apply
Disabled Toilets: Available in the Social Club
Contact: (01492) 514680 (Bookings are not necessary)

Travelling Supporters' Information:
Routes: From Queensferry: Take the A55 and when the expressway is reached take Junction 22 (signposted Old Colwyn). Turn left at the bottom of the slip road then straight on at the mini-roundabout into Llanelian Road. The ground is ½ mile on the right.

GAINSBOROUGH TRINITY FC

Founded: 1873
Former Names: None
Nickname: 'The Blues'
Ground: Northolme, Gainsborough, Lincolnshire, DN21 2QW
Record Attendance: 9,760 (1948)
Pitch Size: 111 × 71 yards

Colours: Blue shirts and shorts
Telephone Nº: (01427) 613295
Clubhouse Phone Nº: (01427) 613688
Fax Number: (01427) 613295
Ground Capacity: 4,340
Seating Capacity: 504
Web site: www.gainsboroughtrinity.com

GENERAL INFORMATION

Car Parking: Street parking and also in a Local Authority Car Park 150 yards from the ground towards the Town Centre
Coach Parking: Available by prior arrangement
Nearest Railway Station: Lea Road (2 miles)
Nearest Bus Station: Heaton Street (1 mile)
Club Shop: At the ground
Opening Times: Matchdays only
Telephone Nº: (01427) 611612

GROUND INFORMATION

Away Supporters' Entrances & Sections:
No usual segregation

ADMISSION INFO (2013/2014 PRICES)

Adult Standing: £11.00
Adult Seating: £12.00
Concessionary Standing: £7.00
Concessionary Seating: £8.00
Under-16s Standing/Seating: £4.00
Under-15s Standing/Seating: Free of charge

DISABLED INFORMATION

Wheelchairs: Accommodated
Helpers: Please phone the club for information
Prices: Normal prices for the disabled. Free for helpers
Disabled Toilets: Available in new block adjacent to the Main Stand
Contact: (01427) 613295   (Bookings are not necessary)

Travelling Supporters' Information:
Routes: From the North, South and West: Exit the A1 at Blyth services taking the 1st left through to Bawtry. In Bawtry, turn right at the traffic lights onto the A631 straight through to Gainsborough (approx. 11 miles). Go over the bridge to the second set of traffic lights and turn left onto the A159 (Scunthorpe Road). Follow the main road past Tesco on the right through the traffic lights. The ground is situated on right approximately a third of a mile north of the Town Centre; From the East: Take the A631 into Gainsborough and turn right onto the A159. Then as above.

GLOUCESTER CITY FC |

Gloucester City are groundsharing with Cheltenham Town FC for the 2013/2014 season.

Founded: 1889 **(Re-formed**: 1980)
Forner Names: Gloucester YMCA
Nickname: 'The Tigers'
Ground: Abbey Business Stadium, Whaddon Road,
Cheltenham, Gloucestershire GL52 5NA
Ground Capacity: 7,136
Seating Capacity: 4,054

Record Attendance: 8,326 (1956)
Pitch Size: 110 × 72 yards
Colours: Yellow and Black Striped shirts, Black shorts
Telephone Nº: 07813 931781
Web Site: www.gloucestercityafc.com
E-mail: contact@gloucestercityafc.com

GENERAL INFORMATION
Car Parking: Very limited parking available at the ground.
A Park & Ride scheme runs from Cheltenham Race Course and
other car parks are available in Cheltenham Town Centre
Coach Parking: At the ground
Nearest Railway Station: Cheltenham Spa (2½ miles)
Nearest Bus Station: Cheltenham Royal Well
Club Shop: At the ground
Opening Times: Matchdays only
GROUND INFORMATION
Away Supporters' Entrances & Sections:
No usual segregation

ADMISSION INFO (2013/2014 PRICES)
Adult Standing: £12.00
Adult Seating: £12.00
Child Standing: £6.00
Child Seating: £6.00
Concessionary Standing: £6.00
Concessionary Seating: £6.00
DISABLED INFORMATION
Wheelchairs: Accommodated in front of the Stagecoach
West Stand (use main entrance) and in the In 2 Print Stand
Helpers: Admitted free of charge
Prices: Normal prices apply for disabled fans
Disabled Toilets: Available in the In 2 Print Stand, adjacent
to the Stagecoach West Stand and in the Social Club
Contact: 07813 931781

Travelling Supporters' Information:
Routes: The ground is situated to the North-East of Cheltenham, 1 mile from the Town Centre off the B4632 (Prestbury Road)
– Whaddon Road is to the East of the B4632 just North of Pittville Circus. Road signs in the vicinity indicate 'Whaddon Road/
Cheltenham Town FC'.

GUISELEY AFC

Founded: 1909
Former Names: None
Nickname: 'The Lions'
Ground: Nethermoor Park, Otley Road, Guiseley, Leeds LS20 8BT
Record Attendance: 2,486 (1989/90)
Pitch Size: 110 × 69 yards

Colours: White shirts with Navy Blue shorts
Telephone Nº: (01943) 873223
Social Club Phone Nº: (01943) 872872
Fax Number: (01943) 873223
Ground Capacity: 3,000
Seating Capacity: 300
Web site: www.guiseleyafc.co.uk
E-mail: admin@guiseleyafc.co.uk

GENERAL INFORMATION

Car Parking: At the ground and in Ings Crescent
Coach Parking: At the ground
Nearest Railway Station: Guiseley (5 minute walk)
Nearest Bus Station: Bus Stop outside the ground
Club Shop: At the ground
Opening Times: Matchdays only
Telephone Nº: (01943) 879236 (weekdays)
Postal Sales: Yes

GROUND INFORMATION

Away Supporters' Entrances & Sections:
No usual segregation

ADMISSION INFO (2013/2014 PRICES)

Adult Standing: £10.00
Adult Seating: £10.00
Under-12s Standing: £2.00
Under-12s Seating: £2.00
Concessionary Standing: £6.00
Concessionary Seating: £6.00

DISABLED INFORMATION

Wheelchairs: Accommodated by the Players' Entrance
Helpers: Admitted
Prices: Free for both disabled fans and helpers
Disabled Toilets: None
Contact: (01943) 879236 (Bookings are advisable)

Travelling Supporters' Information:
Routes: Exit the M62 at Junction 28 and take the Leeds Ring Road to the roundabout at the junction of the A65 at Horsforth. Turn left onto the A65 and pass through Rawdon to Guiseley keeping Morrison's supermarket on your left. Pass straight through the traffic lights with the Station pub or your right and the ground is on the right after ¼ mile, adjacent to the cricket field.

HARROGATE TOWN FC

Founded: 1919
Former Names: Harrogate FC and Harrogate Hotspurs FC
Nickname: 'Town'
Ground: CNG Stadium, Wetherby Road, Harrogate, HG2 7SA
Record Attendance: 4,280 (1950)
Pitch Size: 107 × 72 yards

Colours: Yellow and Black striped shirts, Black shorts
Telephone Nº: (01423) 880675
Club Fax Number: (01423) 883671
Ground Capacity: 3,290
Seating Capacity: 502
Web site: www.harrogatetown.com
E-mail: enquiries@harrogatetown.com

GENERAL INFORMATION

Car Parking: Hospital Car Park adjacent
Coach Parking: At the ground
Nearest Railway Station: Harrogate (¾ mile)
Nearest Bus Station: Harrogate
Club Shop: At the ground
Opening Times: Monday to Friday 9.00am to 3.00pm and also on Matchdays
Telephone Nº: (01423) 885525

GROUND INFORMATION

Away Supporters' Entrances & Sections:
No usual segregation

ADMISSION INFO (2013/2014 PRICES)

Adult Standing: £12.00
Adult Seating: £12.00
Concessionary Standing/Seating: £7.00
Student Standing/Seating: £5.00
Under-16s Standing: £3.00 (when with a paying adult)
Under-16s Seating: £3.00 (when with a paying adult)
Note: Under-5s are admitted free of charge

DISABLED INFORMATION

Wheelchairs: Accommodated at the front of the Main Stand
Helpers: One helper admitted for each disabled fan
Prices: Free of charge for each disabled fan and helper
Disabled Toilets: Available
Contact: (01423) 880675 (Bookings are necessary)

Travelling Supporters' Information:
Routes: From the South: Take the A61 from Leeds and turn right at the roundabout onto the ring road (signposted York). After about 1¼ miles turn left at the next roundabout onto A661 Wetherby Road. The ground is situated ¾ mile on the right; From the West: Take the A59 straight into Wetherby Road from Empress Roundabout and the ground is on the left; From the East & North: Exit the A1(M) at Junction 47, take the A59 to Harrogate then follow the Southern bypass to Wetherby Road for the A661 Roundabout. Turn right towards Harrogate Town Centre and the ground is on the right after ¾ mile.

HEDNESFORD TOWN FC

Founded: 1880
Former Names: Formed by the amalgamation of West Hill FC and Hill Top FC
Nickname: 'The Pitmen'
Ground: Keys Park, Keys Park Road, Hednesford, Cannock WS12 2DZ
Record Attendance: 4,412 (11th May 2013)

Colours: White shirts with Black shorts and socks
Telephone Nº: (01543) 422870
Fax Number: (01543) 428180
Ground Capacity: 6,039
Seating Capacity: 1,011
Pitch Size: 110 × 70 yards
Web site: www.hednesfordtownfc.com

GENERAL INFORMATION

Car Parking: 500 spaces available at the ground – £1.00 fee
Coach Parking: At the ground
Nearest Railway Station: Hednesford (1 mile)
Nearest Bus Station: Hednesford
Club Shop: At the ground
Opening Times: Matchdays and Weekdays from 10.00am to 4.00pm
Telephone Nº: (01543) 422870

GROUND INFORMATION

Away Supporters' Entrances & Sections:
No usual segregation

ADMISSION INFO (2013/2014 PRICES)

Adult Standing: £11.00
Adult Seating: £12.00
Concessionary Standing: £6.00
Concessionary Seating: £7.00
Note: A selection of family tickets are also available
Programme Price: £2.00

DISABLED INFORMATION

Wheelchairs: 8 spaces available in front of the Main Stand
Helpers: Please contact the club for details
Prices: Please contact the club for details
Disabled Toilets: 2 are available – one in the Main Building, one in the Hednesford End of the stand
Contact: (01543) 422870   (Bookings are necessary)

Travelling Supporters' Information:
Routes: Exit the M6 at Junction 11 or the M6 Toll T7 and follow signs for A460 (Rugeley). After crossing the A5 at Churchbridge Island, continue on the A460. After five traffic islands pick up signs for Hednesford Town FC/Keys Park and follow to the ground.

HISTON FC

Founded: 1904
Former Names: Histon Institute FC
Nickname: 'The Stutes'
Ground: The Glass World Stadium, Bridge Road, Impington, Cambridge CB24 9PH
Record Attendance: 6,400 (1956)
Pitch Size: 110 × 75 yards

Colours: Red and Black striped shirts, Black shorts
Telephone Nº: (01223) 237373
Fax Number: (01223) 237495
Ground Capacity: 4,004
Seating Capacity: 1,626
Web site: www.histonfc.co.uk
E-mail: enquiries@histonfc.co.uk

GENERAL INFORMATION

Car Parking: Permit holders and disabled parking only at the ground. Check web site for details of fans parking
Coach Parking: For team coaches only
Nearest Railway Station: Cambridge (4 miles)
Nearest Bus Station: Cambridge (4 miles) (Use Citi 8 service for the ground)
Club Shop: At the ground
Opening Times: Three hours prior to kick-off for both Saturday and evening matches.
Telephone Nº: (01223) 237373

GROUND INFORMATION

Away Supporters' Entrances & Sections:
No usual segregation

ADMISSION INFO (2013/2014 PRICES)

Adult Standing: £11.00
Adult Seating: £11.00
Child Standing: £3.50
Child Seating: £3.50
Under-5s Standing/Seating: Free of charge
Senior Citizen Standing/Seating: £7.00

DISABLED INFORMATION

Wheelchairs: 6 spaces available in the home section and 6 spaces available in the away section
Helpers: Admitted
Prices: Normal prices apply for the disabled. Free for helpers
Disabled Toilets: Available in both the home and away sections
Contact: Mac McDonald (Club safety officer) 07730 557021

Travelling Supporters' Information:
Routes: Exit the M11 at Junction 14 and follow the A14 eastwards. Take the first exit onto the B1049 (signposted Histon & Cottenham). Turn left at the traffic lights at the top of the slip road and pass the Holiday Inn on the right. Continue over the bridge and the entrance to the ground is on the right.

LEAMINGTON FC

Founded: 1891
Former Names: Leamington Town FC, Lockheed Borg & Beck FC, AP Leamington FC and Lockheed Leamington FC
Nickname: 'The Brakes'
Ground: New Windmill Ground, Harbury Lane, Whitnash, Leamington   CV33 9JR

Record Attendance: 1,380 (17th February 2007)
Colours: Gold and Black shirts with Black shorts
Telephone Nº: (01926) 430406
Fax Number: (01926) 430406
Ground Capacity: 5,000
Seating Capacity: 120
Web Site: www.leamingtonfc.co.uk

GENERAL INFORMATION

Car Parking: At the ground
Coach Parking: At the ground
Nearest Railway Station: Leamington (4 miles)
Club Shop: Please contact the club for information
Opening Times: –
Telephone Nº: –

GROUND INFORMATION

Away Supporters' Entrances & Sections:
No usual segregation

ADMISSION INFO (2013/2014 PRICES)

Adult Standing/Seating: £11.00
Concessionary Standing/Seating: £7.00
Under-16s Standing/Seating: £3.00 (Under-12s free)
Student Standing/Seating: £5.00

DISABLED INFORMATION

Wheelchairs: Accommodated
Helpers: Admitted
Prices: Normal prices apply for the disabled. Helpers are admitted free of charge
Disabled Toilets: Available
Contact: (01926) 430406   (Bookings are not necessary)

Travelling Supporters' Information:
Routes: Exit the M40 at Junction 14 and take the A452 towards Leamington continuing at the roundabout into Europa Way (still A452). After approximately ½ mile, take the 4th exit at the roundabout into Harbury Lane (signposted for Harbury and Bishops Tachbrook). Continue on Harbury lane, taking the 3rd exit at the first roundabout and going straight ahead at the traffic lights. The ground is on the left hand side of the road after approximately 1½ miles.

NORTH FERRIBY UNITED FC

Founded: 1934
Former Names: None
Nickname: 'Villagers' or 'Green & Whites'
Ground: Rapid Solicitors Stadium, Church Road, North Ferriby, East Yorkshire HU14 3AB
Record Attendance: 2,000 (vs Hull City in 2009)
Pitch Size: 109 × 76 yards

Colours: White shirts with Green trim, Green shorts
Telephone N°: (01482) 634601
Fax Number: (01482) 634601
Ground Capacity: 2,500
Seating Capacity: 250
Web site: www.northferribyunited.com

GENERAL INFORMATION

Car Parking: Limited spaces at the ground
Coach Parking: At the ground
Nearest Railway Station: Ferriby (5 minutes walk)
Nearest Bus Station: Hull
Club Shop: At the ground
Opening Times: Matchdays only
Telephone N°: (01482) 634601

GROUND INFORMATION

Away Supporters' Entrances & Sections:
No usual segregation

ADMISSION INFO (2013/2014 PRICES)

Adult Standing: £10.00
Adult Seating: £10.00
Senior Citizen/Under-16s Standing: £5.00
Senior Citizen/Under-16s Seating: £5.00
Programme Price: £2.00

DISABLED INFORMATION

Wheelchairs: Accommodated
Helpers: Admitted
Prices: Standard prices apply
Disabled Toilets: Available
Contact: (01482) 634601 (Bookings are not necessary)

Travelling Supporters' Information:
Routes: North Ferriby is approximately 8 miles to the west of Hull on the A63. Upon reaching North Ferriby (from the West), proceed through the village past the Duke of Cumberland Hotel and turn right into Church Lane. The ground is situated on the left after half a mile.

OXFORD CITY FC

Founded: 1882
Former Names: None
Nickname: 'City'
Ground: Oxford City Stadium, Marsh Lane, Marston, Oxford   OX3 0NQ
Record Attendance: 9,500 (1950)

Colours: Blue & White hooped shirts with Blue shorts
Telephone Nº: (01865) 744493 or 07817 885396
Ground Capacity: 3,000
Seating Capacity: 300
Web Site: www.oxfordcityfc.co.uk

GENERAL INFORMATION

Car Parking: At the ground
Coach Parking: At the ground
Nearest Railway Station: Oxford (3¾ miles)
Club Shop: At the ground
Opening Times: Matchdays only
Telephone Nº: (01865) 744493

GROUND INFORMATION

Away Supporters' Entrances & Sections:
No usual segregation

ADMISSION INFO (2013/2014 PRICES)

Adult Standing: £11.00
Adult Seating: £11.00
Concessionary Standing: £6.00
Concessionary Seating: £6.00
Under-16s Standing: Free of charge
Under-16s Seating: Free of charge

DISABLED INFORMATION

Wheelchairs: Accommodated
Helpers: Admitted
Prices: Normal prices apply for the disabled and helpers
Disabled Toilets: Available
Contact: (01865) 744493   (Bookings are not necessary)

Travelling Supporters' Information:
Routes: The stadium is located by the side of the A40 Northern Bypass Road next to the Marston flyover junction to the north east of Oxford. Exit the A40 at the Marston junction and head into Marsh Lane (B4150). Take the first turn on the left into the OXSRAD Complex then turn immediately left again to follow the approach road to the stadium in the far corner of the site.

SOLIHULL MOORS FC

Founded: 2007
Former Names: Formed by the merger of Solihull Borough FC and Moor Green FC in 2007
Nickname: 'The Moors'
Ground: Damson Park, Damson Parkway, Solihull, B91 2PP
Record Attendance: 2,000 (vs Birmingham City)
Pitch Size: 110 × 75 yards

Colours: White shirts with Black shorts
Telephone Nº: (0121) 705-6770
Fax Number: (0121) 711-4045
Ground Capacity: 3,050
Seating Capacity: 280
Web site: www.solihullmoorsfc.co.uk
E-mail: robin.lamb5@btinternet.com

GENERAL INFORMATION
Car Parking: At the ground
Coach Parking: At the ground
Nearest Railway Station: Birmingham International (2 miles)
Nearest Bus Station: Birmingham (5 miles)
Club Shop: At the ground
Opening Times: Matchdays only
Telephone Nº: (0121) 705-6770

GROUND INFORMATION
Away Supporters' Entrances & Sections:
No usual segregation

ADMISSION INFO (2013/2014 PRICES)
Adult Standing: £9.00
Adult Seating: £9.00
Senior Citizen/Junior Standing: £5.00
Senior Citizen/Junior Seating: £5.00

DISABLED INFORMATION
Wheelchairs: Spaces for 3 wheelchairs are available
Helpers: Admitted
Prices: Normal prices apply
Disabled Toilets: Available
Contact: (0121) 705-6770

Travelling Supporters' Information:
Routes: Exit the M42 at Junction 6 and take the A45 for 2 miles towards Birmingham. Turn left at the traffic lights near the Posthouse Hotel into Damson Parkway (signposted for Landrover/Damsonwood). Continue to the roundabout and come back along the other carriageway to the ground which is situated on the left after about 150 yards.

STALYBRIDGE CELTIC FC

Founded: 1909	**Colours**: Blue shirts, White shorts and Blue socks
Former Names: None	**Telephone N°**: (0161) 338-2828
Nickname: 'Celtic'	**Daytime Phone N°**: (0161) 338-2828
Ground: Bower Fold, Mottram Road, Stalybridge,	**Fax Number**: (0161) 338-8256
Cheshire SK15 2RT	**Ground Capacity**: 6,108 **Seating Capacity**: 1,155
Record Attendance: 9,753 (1922/23)	**Web site**: www.stalybridgeceltic.co.uk
Pitch Size: 109 × 70 yards	**E-mail**: office@stalybridgeceltic.co.uk

GENERAL INFORMATION

Car Parking: At the ground (£1.00 charge)
Coach Parking: At the ground
Nearest Railway Station: Stalybridge (1 mile)
Nearest Bus Station: Stalybridge town centre
Club Shop: At the ground and also at "Stitch in Time", Market Street, Stalybridge
Opening Times: Matchdays only at the ground
Monday to Friday 9.00am to 5.00pm at Market Street
Telephone N°: (0161) 338-2828

GROUND INFORMATION

Away Supporters' Entrances & Sections:
Lockwood & Greenwood Stand on the few occasions when segregation is required. No usual segregation

ADMISSION INFO (2013/2014 PRICES)

Adult Standing: £10.00
Adult Seating: £10.00
Concessionary Standing: £6.00
Concessionary Seating: £6.00
Note: Under-12s are admitted for £1.00 when accompanied by a paying adult

DISABLED INFORMATION

Wheelchairs: 20 spaces available each for home and away fans at the side of the Stepan Stand. A further 9 spaces available in the new Lord Tom Pendry Stand
Helpers: Please phone the club for information
Prices: Please phone the club for information
Disabled Toilets: Available at the rear of the Stepan Stand and at the side of the Lord Tom Pendry Stand
Contact: (0161) 338-2828 (Bookings are necessary)

Travelling Supporters' Information:
Routes: From the Midlands and South: Take the M6, M56, M60 and M67, leaving at the end of the motorway. Go across the roundabout to the traffic lights and turn left. The ground is approximately 2 miles on the left before the Hare & Hounds pub; From the North: Exit the M62 at Junction 18 onto the M60 singposted for Ashton-under-Lyne. Follow the M60 to Junction 24 and join the M67, then as from the Midlands and South.

STOCKPORT COUNTY FC

Founded: 1883
Former Names: Heaton Norris Rovers FC
Nickname: 'Hatters' 'County'
Ground: Edgeley Park, Hardcastle Road, Edgeley, Stockport SK3 9DD
Ground Capacity: 10,641 (All seats)
Record Attendance: 27,833 (11th February 1950)
Pitch Size: 111 × 72 yards

Colours: Blue shirts with White shorts
Telephone Nº: (0161) 2868888
Ticket Office: 0845 688-5799
Fax Number: (0161) 429-7392
Web Site: www.stockportcounty.com
E-mail: fans@stockportcounty.com

GENERAL INFORMATION
Car Parking: Booth Street (nearby) £4.00
Coach Parking: Booth Street (£20.00)
Nearest Railway Station: Stockport (5 minutes walk)
Nearest Bus Station: Mersey Square (10 minutes walk)
Club Shop: At the ground
Opening Times: Monday to Friday from 9.00am – 4.00pm. Open until 7.30pm on matchdays during the week and also on Saturday matchdays 10.00am – 2.45pm then for 30 minutes after the game.
Telephone Nº: (0161) 474-0310

GROUND INFORMATION
Away Supporters' Entrances & Sections:
Railway End turnstiles for Railway End or turnstiles for Popular Side depending on the opponents

ADMISSION INFO (2013/2014 PRICES)
Adult Seating: £15.00
Under-22s Seating: £11.00
Under-17s Seating: £3.00
Under-10s Seating: £1.00
Senior Citizen Seating: £10.00

DISABLED INFORMATION
Wheelchairs: 16 spaces in total. 10 in the Hardcastle Road Stand, 6 in the Cheadle Stand
Helpers: One helper admitted per disabled fan
Prices: £10.00 for the disabled. Helpers free of charge
Disabled Toilets: Yes
Contact: 0845 688-5799 (Bookings are necessary)

Travelling Supporters' Information:
Routes: From the North, South and West: Exit the M63 at Junction 11 and join the A560, following signs for Cheadle. After ¼ mile turn right into Edgeley Road and after 1 mile turn right into Caroline Street for the ground; From the East: Take the A6 or A560 into Stockport Town Centre and turn left into Greek Street. Take the 2nd exit into Mercian Way (from the roundabout) then turn left into Caroline Street – the ground is straight ahead.

VAUXHALL MOTORS FC

Founded: 1963
Former Names: Vauxhall GM FC
Nickname: 'Motormen'
Ground: Rivacre Park, Rivacre Road, Hooton, Ellesmere Port, Cheshire   CH66 1NJ
Record Attendance: 1,752 (2012)
Pitch Size: 117 × 78 yards

Colours: White shirts with Blue shorts
Telephone N°: (0151) 328-1114 (Ground)
Fax N°: (0151) 328-1114
Ground Capacity: 3,306
Seating Capacity: 266
Web site: www.vmfc.com

GENERAL INFORMATION
Car Parking: At the ground
Coach Parking: At the ground
Nearest Railway Station: Overpool
Nearest Bus Station: Ellesmere Port
Club Shop: At the ground
Opening Times: Matchdays only
Telephone N°: None

GROUND INFORMATION
Away Supporters' Entrances & Sections:
No usual segregation

ADMISSION INFO (2013/2014 PRICES)
Adult Standing: £10.00
Adult Seating: £10.00
Child Standing: £2.00
Child Seating: £2.00
Senior Citizen Standing/Seating: £6.00
Student Standing/Seating: £6.00

DISABLED INFORMATION
Wheelchairs: Accommodated as necessary
Helpers: Admitted
Prices: Normal prices for the disabled. Free for carers
Disabled Toilets: Available
Contact: –   (Bookings are not necessary)

Travelling Supporters' Information:
Routes: Exit the M53 at Junction 5 and take the A41 towards Chester. Turn left at the first set of traffic lights into Hooton Green. Turn left at the first T-junction then right at the next T-junction into Rivacre Road. The ground is situated 250 yards on the right.

WORCESTER CITY FC

Worcester City FC are groundsharing with Kidderminster Harriers FC during the 2013/2014 season.

Founded: 1902
Former Names: Berwick Rangers FC
Nickname: 'The City'
Ground: Aggborough, Hoo Road, Kidderminster, Worcestershire   DY10 1NB
Ground Capacity: 6,444   **Seating Capacity**: 3,143
Record Attendance: 9,155 (1948)

Pitch Size: 110 × 72 yards
Colours: Blue and White shirts with Blue shorts
Telephone Nº: (01905) 23003
Fax Number: (01905) 26668
Web site: www.worcestercityfc.co.uk
E-mail: office@worcestercityfc.co.uk

GENERAL INFORMATION

Car Parking: At the ground
Coach Parking: As directed
Nearest Railway Station: Kidderminster
Nearest Bus Station: Kidderminster Town Centre
Club Shop: Online sales only at present
Telephone Nº: (01905) 23003

GROUND INFORMATION

Away Supporters' Entrances & Sections:
John Smiths Stand Entrance D and South Terrace Entrance E

ADMISSION INFO (2013/2014 PRICES)

Adult Standing: £12.00
Adult Seating: £14.00
Under-16s Standing: £3.00
Under-16s Seating: £5.00
Young Adult Standing: £5.00
Young Adult Seating: £7.00
Senior Citizen Standing: £8.00
Senior Citizen Seating: £10.00

DISABLED INFORMATION

Wheelchairs: Home fans accommodated at the front of the Main Stand, Away fans in front of the John Smiths Stand
Helpers: Admitted
Prices: Please contact the club for further information
Disabled Toilets: Available by the disabled area
Contact: (01905) 23003   (Bookings are necessary)

Travelling Supporters' Information:
Routes: Exit the M5 at Junction 3 and follow the A456 to Kidderminster. The ground is situated close by the Severn Valley Railway Station so follow the brown Steam Train signs and turn into Hoo Road about 200 yards downhill of the station. Follow the road along for ¼ mile and the ground is on the left.

WORKINGTON AFC

Founded: 1884 (Reformed 1921)
Former Names: None
Nickname: 'Reds'
Ground: Borough Park, Workington   CA14 2DT
Record Attendance: 21,000 (vs Manchester United)
Pitch Size: 112 × 72 yards

Colours: Red shirts with White shorts
Telephone Nº: (01900) 602871
Fax Number: (01900) 67432
Ground Capacity: 3,100
Seating Capacity: 500
Web site: www.workingtonafc.com
E-mail: workington.reds@tiscali.co.uk

GENERAL INFORMATION

Car Parking: Car Park next to the ground
Coach Parking: At the ground
Nearest Railway Station: Workington (¼ mile)
Nearest Bus Station: Workington (½ mile)
Club Shop: At the ground
Opening Times: Matchdays only
Telephone Nº: (01946) 832710

GROUND INFORMATION

Away Supporters' Entrances & Sections:
No usual segregation

ADMISSION INFO (2013/2014 PRICES)

Adult Standing/Seating: £12.00
Concessionary Standing/Seating: £7.00
Under-16s Standing/Seating: £5.00

DISABLED INFORMATION

Wheelchairs: Accommodated
Helpers: Admitted
Prices: Normal prices apply
Disabled Toilets: Available
Contact: (01900) 602871   (Bookings are not necessary)

Travelling Supporters' Information:
Routes: Exit the M6 at Junction 40 and take the A66 towards Keswick and Workington. Upon reaching Workington, continue until you reach the traffic lights at the bottom of the hill (with HSBC Bank facing) and turn left towards the town centre. Approach the traffic lights in the middle lane with the Washington Central Hotel on the right and turn right. Continue along this road, crossing a mini-roundabout, a pedestrian crossing and a further set of traffic lights. Upon reaching the railway station, pass through the junction and bear right passing the Derwent Park Rugby League Stadium then bear left and Borough Park is straight ahead.

THE FOOTBALL CONFERENCE SOUTH

Address

Third Floor, Wellington House,
31-34 Waterloo Street, Birmingham   B2 5TJ

Phone (0121) 214-1950

Web site   www.footballconference.co.uk

Clubs for the 2013/2014 Season

BASINGSTOKE TOWN FC

Founded: 1896
Former Names: None
Nickname: 'Dragons'
Ground: The Camrose Ground, Western Way, Basingstoke, Hants. RG22 6EZ
Record Attendance: 5,085 (25th November 1997)
Pitch Size: 110 × 70 yards

Colours: Yellow and Blue shirts with Blue shorts
Telephone Nº: (01256) 327575
Fax Number: (01256) 326346
Social Club Nº: (01256) 464353
Ground Capacity: 6,000
Seating Capacity: 650
Web site: www.basingstoketown.net
E-mail: richard.trodd@ntlworld.com

GENERAL INFORMATION

Car Parking: 600 spaces available at the ground (£1.00)
Coach Parking: Ample room available at ground
Nearest Railway Station: Basingstoke
Nearest Bus Station: Basingstoke Town Centre (2 miles)
Club Shop: The Camrose Shop
Opening Times: Matchdays only
Telephone Nº: (01256) 327575

GROUND INFORMATION

Away Supporters' Entrances & Sections:
No usual segregation

ADMISSION INFO (2013/2014 PRICES)

Adult Standing: £12.00
Adult Seating: £13.00
Concessionary Standing: £8.00
Concessionary Seating: £9.00
Under-16s Standing: £4.00
Under-16s Seating: £5.00
Under-11s Standing: £2.00
Under-11s Seating: £3.00

DISABLED INFORMATION

Wheelchairs: 6 spaces are available under cover
Helpers: Admitted
Prices: Normal prices for the disabled. Free for helpers
Disabled Toilets: Yes
Contact: (01256) 327575 (Bookings are not necessary)

Travelling Supporters' Information:
Routes: Exit the M3 at Junction 6 and take the 1st left at the Black Dam roundabout. At the next roundabout take the 2nd exit, then the 1st exit at the following roundabout and the 5th exit at the next roundabout. This takes you into Western Way and the ground is 50 yards on the right.

BATH CITY FC

Founded: 1889
Former Names: Bath AFC, Bath Railway FC and Bath Amateurs FC
Nickname: 'The Romans'
Ground: Twerton Park, Bath   BA2 1DB
Record Attendance: 18,020 (1960)
Pitch Size: 110 × 76 yards

Colours: Black and White striped shirts, Black shorts
Telephone Nº: (01225) 423087/313247
Fax Number: (01225) 481391
Ground Capacity: 8,840
Seating Capacity: 1,026
Web site: www.bathcityfc.com

GENERAL INFORMATION
Car Parking: 150 spaces available at the ground
Coach Parking: Available at the ground
Nearest Railway Station: Oldfield Park (1 mile)
Nearest Bus Station: Avon Street, Bath
Club Shop: Yes – contact Andy Weeks, c/o Club
Opening Times: Matchdays and office hours
Telephone Nº: (01225) 423087

GROUND INFORMATION
Away Supporters' Entrances & Sections:
Turnstiles 17-19

ADMISSION INFO (2013/2014 PRICES)
Adult Standing: £12.00
Adult Seating: £13.00
Senior Citizen Standing: £8.00
Senior Citizen Seating: £9.00
Under-16s Standing: £3.00
Under-16s Seating: £4.00

DISABLED INFORMATION
Wheelchairs: 10 spaces available each for home and away fans in front of the Family Stand
Helpers: Admitted
Prices: Normal prices for the disabled. Free for helpers
Disabled Toilets: Available behind the Family Stand
Contact: (01225) 423087   (Bookings are necessary)

Travelling Supporters' Information:
Route: As a recommendation, avoid exiting the M4 at Junction 18 as the road from takes you through Bath City Centre. Instead, exit the M4 at Junction 19 onto the M32. Turn off the M32 at Junction 1 and follow the A4174 Bristol Ring Road south then join the A4 for Bath. On the A4, after passing through Saltford you will reach a roundabout shortly before entering Bath. Take the 2nd exit at this roundabout then follow the road before turning left into Newton Road at the bottom of the steep hill. The ground is then on the right hand side of the road.

BISHOP'S STORTFORD FC |

Founded: 1874
Former Names: None
Nickname: 'Blues' 'Bishops'
Ground: Woodside Park, Dunmow Road,
Bishop's Stortford   CM23 5RG
Record Attendance: 3,555 (2000)
Pitch Size: 110 × 70 yards

Colours: Blue and White shirts with Blue shorts
Telephone No: (01279) 306456
Fax Number: (01279) 715621
Ground Capacity: 4,000
Seating Capacity: 500
Web site: www.bsfc.co.uk

GENERAL INFORMATION
Car Parking: 500 spaces available at the ground
Coach Parking: At the ground
Nearest Railway Station: Bishop's Stortford
Nearest Bus Station: Bishop's Stortford
Club Shop: At the ground
Opening Times: Matchdays only 1.30pm to 5.00pm
Telephone No: (01279) 306456

GROUND INFORMATION
Away Supporters' Entrances & Sections:
No usual segregation

ADMISSION INFO (2013/2014 PRICES)
Adult Standing/Seating: £12.00
Concessionary Standing/Seating: £7.00
Student Standing/Seating: £6.00
Under-16s Standing/Seating: £5.00
Note: Under-12s are admitted free of charge when
accompanied by a paying adult.

DISABLED INFORMATION
Wheelchairs: Accommodated in the disabled section
Helpers: Admitted
Prices: Free of charge for the disabled and helpers
Disabled Toilets: Yes
Contact: (01279) 306456   (Bookings are not necessary)

Travelling Supporters' Information:
Routes: Exit the M11 at junction 8 and take the A1250 towards Bishop Stortford. Turn left at the first roundabout and the ground is first right opposite the Golf Club (the entrance is between Industrial Units).

BOREHAM WOOD FC

Founded: 1948
Former Names: Boreham Rovers FC and Royal Retournez FC
Nickname: 'The Wood'
Ground: Meadow Park, Broughinge Road, Boreham Wood, Hertfordshire WD6 5AL
Record Attendance: 4,030 (2002)
Pitch Size: 112 × 72 yards

Colours: White shirts with Black shorts
Telephone Nº: (0208) 953-5097
Fax Number: (0208) 207-7982
Ground Capacity: 4,239
Seating Capacity: 500
Web site: www.borehamwoodfootballclub.co.uk

GENERAL INFORMATION

Car Parking: At the ground
Coach Parking: At the ground
Nearest Railway Station: Elstree & Boreham Wood (1 mile)
Nearest Bus Station: Barnet
Club Shop: At the ground
Opening Times: 11.00am to 10.00pm Monday to Thursday; 11.00am to 6.00pm at weekends
Telephone Nº: (0208) 953-5097

GROUND INFORMATION

Away Supporters' Entrances & Sections:
No usual segregation

ADMISSION INFO (2013/2014 PRICES)

Adult Standing: £12.00
Adult Seating: £12.00
Child Standing: £6.00
Child Seating: £6.00

DISABLED INFORMATION

Wheelchairs: Accommodated
Helpers: Admitted
Prices: Concessionary prices are charged for the disabled and helpers
Disabled Toilets: None
Contact: (0208) 953-5097   (Bookings are necessary)

Travelling Supporters' Information:
Routes: Exit the M25 at Junction 23 and take the A1 South. After 2 miles, take the Boreham Wood exit onto the dual carriageway and go over the flyover following signs for Boreham Wood for 1 mile. Turn right at the Studio roundabout into Brook Road, then next right into Broughinge Road for the ground.

BROMLEY FC

Founded: 1892
Former Names: None
Nickname: 'Lillywhites'
Ground: The Stadium, Hayes Lane, Bromley, Kent, BR2 9EF
Record Attendance: 12,000 (24th September 1949)
Pitch Size: 112 × 72 yards

Colours: White shirts with Black shorts
Telephone Nº: (020) 8460-5291
Fax Number: (020) 8313-3992
Ground Capacity: 3,300
Seating Capacity: 1,300
Web site: www.bromleyfc.net
E-mail: info@bromleyfc.net

GENERAL INFORMATION
Car Parking: 300 spaces available at the ground
Coach Parking: At the ground
Nearest Railway Station: Bromley South (1 mile)
Nearest Bus Station: High Street, Bromley
Club Shop: At the ground
Opening Times: Matchdays only
Telephone Nº: (020) 8460-5291

GROUND INFORMATION
Away Supporters' Entrances & Sections:
No usual segregation

ADMISSION INFO (2013/2014 PRICES)
Adult Standing/Seating: £12.00
Concessionary Standing/Seating: £6.00
Under-16s/Student Standing/Seating: £5.00
Note: Under-5s are admitted free of charge

DISABLED INFORMATION
Wheelchairs: Accommodated
Helpers: Admitted
Prices: Please phone the club for information
Disabled Toilets: Yes
Contact: (0181) 460-5291 (Bookings are necessary)

Travelling Supporters' Information:
Routes: Exit the M25 at Junction 4 and follow the A21 for Bromley and London for approximately 4 miles before forking left onto the A232 signposted for Croydon/Sutton. At the second set of traffic lights turn right into Baston Road (B265) and follow for approximately 2 miles as it becomes Hayes Street and then Hayes Lane. The ground is on the right just after a mini-roundabout.

CHELMSFORD CITY FC

Founded: 1938
Former Names: Chelmsford FC
Nickname: 'City' or 'Clarets'
Ground: Melbourne Stadium, Salerno Way, Chelmsford CM1 2EH
Record Attendance: 16,807 (at previous ground)
Pitch Size: 109 × 70 yards

Colours: Claret and White shirts and shorts
Telephone Nº: (01245) 290959
Ground Capacity: 3,000
Seating Capacity: 1,400
Web site: www.chelmsfordcityfc.com

GENERAL INFORMATION

Car Parking: Limited space at ground and street parking
Coach Parking: Two spaces available at the ground subject to advance notice
Nearest Railway Station: Chelmsford (2 miles)
Nearest Bus Station: Chelmsford (2 miles)
Club Shop: At the ground
Opening Times: Matchdays only at present
Telephone Nº: (01245) 290959

GROUND INFORMATION

Away Supporters' Entrances & Sections:
No usual segregation

ADMISSION INFO (2013/2014 PRICES)

Adult Standing: £11.50
Adult Seating: £12.50
Under-16s Standing: £3.50
Under-16s Seating: £4.50
Under-12s Standing: Free of charge
Under-12s Seating: £1.00
Concessionary Standing: £7.50
Concessionary Seating: £8.50

DISABLED INFORMATION

Wheelchairs: Spaces for 11 wheelchairs available
Helpers: Admitted free of charge
Prices: Disabled fans are charged standing admission prices
Disabled Toilets: Available
Contact: (01245) 290959   (Bookings are necessary)

Travelling Supporters' Information:
Route: The ground is situated next to the only set of high rise flats in Chelmsford which can therefore be used as a landmark. From the A12 from London: Exit the A12 at Junction 15 signposted for Chelmsford/Harlow/A414 and head towards Chelmsford along the dual-carriageway. At the third roundabout, immediately after passing the 'Superbowl' on the left, take the first exit into Westway, signposted for the Crematorium and Widford Industrial Estate. Continue along Westway which becomes Waterhouse Lane after the second set of traffic lights. At the next set of lights (at the gyratory system) take the first exit into Rainsford Road, signposted for Sawbridgeworth A1060. Continue along Rainsford Road then turn right into Chignal Road at the second set of traffic lights. Turn right again into Melbourne Avenue and Salerno Way is on the left at the end of the football pitches.

CONCORD RANGERS FC

Founded: 1967
Former Names: None
Nickname: 'Beach Boys'
Ground: Aspect Arena, Thames Road, Canvey Island, SS8 0HH
Record Attendance: 1,500

Colours: Yellow shirts with Blue shorts
Telephone Nº: (01268) 515750
Ground Capacity: 2,000
Seating Capacity: 340
Web Site: www.concordrangers.co.uk

GENERAL INFORMATION

Car Parking: At the ground
Coach Parking: At the ground
Nearest Railway Station: Benfleet
Club Shop: Available via the club's web site shortly
Opening Times: –
Telephone Nº: –

GROUND INFORMATION

Away Supporters' Entrances & Sections:
No usual segregation

ADMISSION INFO (2013/2014 PRICES)

Adult Standing: £12.00
Adult Seating: £12.00
Senior Citizen Standing: £6.00
Senior Citizen Seating: £6.00
Under-16s Standing/Seating: £3.00
Programme Price: £1.00

DISABLED INFORMATION

Wheelchairs: Accommodated
Helpers: Admitted
Prices: Normal prices apply for the disabled and helpers
Disabled Toilets: Available
Contact: (01268) 515750   (Bookings are necessary)

Travelling Supporters' Information:
Routes: Take the A13 to the A130 (Canvey Way) for Canvey Island. At the Benfleet roundabout, take the 3rd exit into Canvey Road and continue along through Charfleets Service Road into Long Road. Take the 5th turn on the right into Thorney Bay Road and Thames Road is the 3rd turn on the right. The ground is on the left-hand side by the oil storage tanks.

DORCHESTER TOWN FC

Founded: 1880
Former Names: None
Nickname: 'The Magpies'
Ground: The Avenue Stadium, Weymouth Avenue, Dorchester, Dorset   DT1 2RY
Record Attendance: 4,159 (1st January 1999)
Pitch Size: 110 × 80 yards

Colours: Black and White striped shirts with Black shorts and socks
Telephone Nº: (01305) 262451
Fax Number: (01305) 267623
Ground Capacity: 5,009
Seating Capacity: 710
Web Site: www.dorchestertownfc.co.uk
E-mail: manager@dorchestertownfc.co.uk

GENERAL INFORMATION

Car Parking: 350 spaces available at the ground (£1.00 fee)
Coach Parking: At the ground
Nearest Railway Station: Dorchester South and West (both 1 mile)
Nearest Bus Station: Nearby
Club Shop: At the ground
Opening Times: During 1st team matchdays only
Telephone Nº: (01305) 262451

GROUND INFORMATION

Away Supporters' Entrances & Sections:
Main Stand side when segregated (not usual)

ADMISSION INFO (2013/2014 PRICES)

Adult Standing: £12.00
Adult Seating: £12.00
Senior Citizen Standing: £8.00
Senior Citizen Seating: £8.00
Junior Standing: £3.00
Junior Seating: £3.00

DISABLED INFORMATION

Wheelchairs: 10 spaces available each for home and away fans at the North West End of the terracing
Helpers: Admitted
Prices: Normal prices apply
Disabled Toilets: 2 available near the disabled area
Contact: (01305) 262451   (Bookings are not necessary)

Travelling Supporters' Information:
Routes: Take the Dorchester Bypass (A35) from all directions. The ground is on the South side of town, adjacent to a roundabout at the intersection with the A354 to Weymouth. Alternatively, take Weymouth signs from Dorchester Town Centre for 1½ miles.

DOVER ATHLETIC FC

Founded: 1983
Former Names: None
Nickname: 'The Whites'
Ground: Crabble Athletic Ground, Lewisham Road, River, Dover   CT17 0JB
Record Attendance: 4,186 (2002)
Pitch Size: 111 × 73 yards

Colours: White shirts with Black shorts
Telephone N°: (01304) 822373
Fax Number: (01304) 821383
Ground Capacity: 6,500
Seating Capacity: 1,000
Web site: www.dover-athletic.com
E-mail: enquiries@doverathletic.com

GENERAL INFORMATION
Car Parking: Street parking
Coach Parking: Street parking
Nearest Railway Station: Kearsney (1 mile)
Nearest Bus Station: Pencester Road, Dover (1½ miles)
Club Shop: At the ground
Opening Times: Saturdays 9.00am to 12.00pm
Telephone N°: (01304) 822373

GROUND INFORMATION
Away Supporters' Entrances & Sections:
Segregation only used when required

ADMISSION INFO (2013/2014 PRICES)
Adult Standing: £13.00
Adult Seating: £13.50
Senior Citizen Standing: £10.00
Senior Citizen Seating: £10.00
Under-18s Standing: £6.00
Under-18s Seating: £6.50
Under-11s Standing/Seating: Free of charge

DISABLED INFORMATION
Wheelchairs: Approximately 20 spaces are available in front of the Family Stand
Helpers: Please phone the club for information
Prices: Please phone the club for information
Disabled Toilets: None
Contact: –   (Bookings are not necessary)

Travelling Supporters' Information:
Routes: Take the A2 to the Whitfield roundabout and take the 4th exit. Travel down the hill to the mini-roundabout then turn left and follow the road for 1 mile to the traffic lights on the hill. Turn sharp right and pass under the railway bridge – the ground is on the left after 300 yards.

EASTBOURNE BOROUGH FC

Founded: 1963
Former Names: Langney Sports FC
Nickname: 'The Sports'
Ground: Langney Sports Club, Priory Lane,
Eastbourne   BN23 7QH
Record Attendance: 3,770   (5th November 2005)
Pitch Size: 115 × 72 yards

Colours: Red shirts with Black shorts
Telephone Nº: (01323) 766265
Fax Number: (01323) 741627
Ground Capacity: 4,400
Seating Capacity: 542
Web site: www.ebfc.co.uk

GENERAL INFORMATION

Car Parking: Around 400 spaces available at the ground
Coach Parking: At the ground
Nearest Railway Station: Pevensey & Westham (1½ miles but no public transport to the ground)
Nearest Bus Station: Eastbourne   (Service 6A to ground)
Club Shop: At the ground
Opening Times: Matchdays only
Telephone Nº: (01323) 766265

GROUND INFORMATION

Away Supporters' Entrances & Sections:
No usual segregation

ADMISSION INFO (2013/2014 PRICES)

Adult Standing: £12.00
Adult Seating: £12.00
Under-16s Standing: £1.00
Under-16s Seating: £1.00
Senior Citizen Standing: £8.00
Senior Citizen Seating: £8.00

DISABLED INFORMATION

Wheelchairs: 6 spaces available
Helpers: Admitted
Prices: Normal prices apply
Disabled Toilets: Available
Contact: (01323) 766265   (Bookings are necessary)

Travelling Supporters' Information:
Routes: From the North: Exit the A22 onto the Polegate bypass, signposted A27 Eastbourne, Hastings & Bexhill. *Take the 2nd exit at the next roundabout for Stone Cross and Westham (A22) then the first exit at the following roundabout signposted Stone Cross and Westham. Turn right after ½ mile into Friday Street (B2104). At the end of Friday Street, turn left at the double mini-roundabout into Hide Hollow (B2191), passing Eastbourne Crematorium on your right. Turn right at the roundabout into Priory Road, and Priory Lane is about 200 yards down the road on the left; Approaching on the A27 from Brighton: Turn left at the Polegate traffic lights then take 2nd exit at the large roundabout to join the bypass. Then as from *.

EASTLEIGH FC

Founded: 1946
Former Names: Swaythling Athletic FC and Swaythling FC
Nickname: 'The Spitfires'
Ground: Silverlake Stadium, Ten Acres, Stoneham Lane, Eastleigh   SO50 9HT
Record Attendance: 3,104 (2006)
Pitch Size: 112 × 74 yards

Colours: Blue shirts with White shorts
Telephone Nº: (023) 8061-3361
Fax Number: (023) 8061-2379
Ground Capacity: 3,000
Seating Capacity: 512
Web site: www.eastleighfc.com
e-mail: rmurphy@eastleighfc.com

GENERAL INFORMATION
Car Parking: Spaces for 450 cars available (hard standing)
Coach Parking: At the ground
Nearest Railway Station: Southampton Parkway (¾ mile)
Nearest Bus Station: Eastleigh (2 miles)
Club Shop: At the ground
Opening Times: Matchdays and during functions only

GROUND INFORMATION
Away Supporters' Entrances & Sections:
No usual segregation

ADMISSION INFO (2013/2014 PRICES)
Adult Standing/Seating: £12.00
Concessionary Standing/Seating: £7.50
Under-16s Standing/Seating: £4.00
Under-12s Standing/Seating: Free of charge

DISABLED INFORMATION
Wheelchairs: Accommodated
Helpers: Admitted
Prices: Normal prices apply
Disabled Toilets: Available
Contact: (023) 8061-3361   (Bookings are not necessary)

Travelling Supporters' Information:
Routes: Exit the M27 at Junction 5 (signposted for Southampton Airport) and take the A335 (Stoneham Way) towards Southampton. After ½ mile, turn right at the traffic lights into Bassett Green Road. Turn right at the next set of traffic lights into Stoneham Lane and the ground is on the right after ¾ mile.

EBBSFLEET UNITED FC

Founded: 1946
Former Names: Gravesend & Northfleet United FC, Gravesend United FC and Northfleet United FC
Nickname: 'The Fleet'
Ground: Stonebridge Road, Northfleet, Gravesend, Kent   DA11 9GN
Record Attendance: 12,063 (1963)
Pitch Size: 112 × 72 yards

Colours: Reds shirts with White shorts
Telephone Nº: (01474) 533796
Fax Number: (01474) 324754
Ground Capacity: 5,258
Seating Capacity: 1,220
Web site: www.ebbsfleetunited.co.uk
E-mail: info@eufc.co.uk

GENERAL INFORMATION
Car Parking: Ebbsfleet International Car Park C (when available) and also street parking
Coach Parking: At the ground
Nearest Railway Station: Northfleet (5 minutes walk)
Nearest Bus Station: Bus Stop outside the ground
Club Shop: At the ground
Opening Times: Matchdays only
Telephone Nº: (01474) 533796

GROUND INFORMATION
Away Supporters' Entrances & Sections:
Only some games are segregated – contact club for details

ADMISSION INFO (2013/2014 PRICES)
Adult Standing: £10.00
Adult Seating: £10.00
Concessionary Standing: £8.00
Concessionary Seating: £8.00
Under-16s Standing/Seating: £5.00
Under-12s Standing/Seating: Free of charge

DISABLED INFORMATION
Wheelchairs: 6 spaces are available in the Disabled Area in front of the Main Stand
Helpers: Admitted free of charge
Prices: Please phone the club for information
Disabled Toilets: Available in the Main Stand
Contact: (01474) 533796   (Bookings are necessary)

Travelling Supporters' Information:
Routes: Take the A2 to the Northfleet/Southfleet exit and follow signs for Northfleet (B262). Go straight on at the first roundabout then take the 2nd exit at the 2nd roundabout into Thames Way and follow the football signs for the ground.

FARNBOROUGH FC

Founded: 1967 (Re-formed in 2007)
Former Names: Farnborough Town FC
Nickname: 'The Boro'
Ground: The Rushmoor Community Stadium, Cherrywood Road, Farnborough GU14 8UD
Record Attendance: 4,267 (15th May 2011)
Pitch Size: 115 × 77 yards

Colours: Yellow and Blue shirts and shorts
Telephone Nº: (01252) 541469
Fax Number: (01252) 372640
Ground Capacity: 5,600 at present
Seating Capacity: 3,135
Web site: www.farnboroughfc.co.uk
E-mail contact: admin@farnboroughfc.co.uk

GENERAL INFORMATION

Car Parking: 260 spaces available at the ground with a further 200 spaces at the nearby Sixth Form college
Coach Parking: At the ground
Nearest Railway Stations: Farnborough (Main), Farnborough North, Frimley and Blackwater
Nearest Bus Station: Buses from Farnborough Main stop just outside the ground – please check the web site for details.
Club Shop: At the ground + web sales in the near future
Opening Times: Matchdays only
Telephone Nº: (01252) 541469

GROUND INFORMATION

Away Supporters' Entrances & Sections:
Moor Road entrances and accommodation

ADMISSION INFO (2013/2014 PRICES)

Adult Standing: £12.00
Adult Seating: £12.00
Concessionary Standing: £8.00
Concessionary Seating: £8.00
Under-16s Seating/Standing: £3.00
Under-6s Seating/Standing: Free of charge
Note: In keeping with F.A. Regulations, the Club reserves the right to charge higher prices for F.A. Trophy and F.A. Cup games.
Programme Price: £2.50

DISABLED INFORMATION

Wheelchairs: Spaces available in a disabled section in the PRE Stand
Helpers: Admitted free of charge
Prices: Concessionary prices charged for disabled fans
Disabled Toilets: Available in the PRE Stand
Contact: 0844 807-9900 (Bookings are not necessary)

Travelling Supporters' Information:
Routes: Exit the M3 at Junction 4 and take the A331 signposted for Farnham. After a few hundred yards exit at the second slip road – signposted A325 Farnborough – turn right at the roundabout and cross over the dual carriageway and a small roundabout. Pass the Farnborough Gate shopping centre on your left and at the next roundabout turn left onto the A325. Go over a pelican crossing and at the next set of lights take the right filter lane into Prospect Avenue. At the end of this road turn right at the roundabout into Cherrywood Road. The ground is on the right after ½ mile.

GOSPORT BOROUGH FC

Founded: 1944
Former Names: Gosport Borough Athletic FC
Nickname: 'The Boro'
Ground: Privett Park, Privett Road, Gosport, PO12 3SX
Record Attendance: 4,770 (1951)

Colours: Yellow shirts with Navy Blue shorts
Telephone Nº: (023) 9250-1042
Fax Number: (01329) 235961
Ground Capacity: 4,500
Seating Capacity: 450
Web Site: www.gosportboroughfc.co.uk

GENERAL INFORMATION
Car Parking: At the ground
Coach Parking: At the ground
Nearest Railway Station: Fareham (5½ miles)
Club Shop: At the ground
Opening Times: Matchdays only
Telephone Nº: –

GROUND INFORMATION
Away Supporters' Entrances & Sections:
No usual segregation

ADMISSION INFO (2013/2014 PRICES)
Adult Standing: £12.00
Adult Seating: £12.00
Concessionary Standing: £8.00
Concessionary Seating: £8.00
Note: Under-10s are admitted free of charge when accompanied by a paying adult

DISABLED INFORMATION
Wheelchairs: Accommodated
Helpers: Admitted
Prices: Normal prices apply for the disabled and helpers
Disabled Toilets: Available
Contact: (023) 9250-1042 (Bookings are not necessary)

Travelling Supporters' Information:
Routes: Exit the M27 at Junction 11 and follow take the A27 Eastern Way towards Gosport. Turn left at the roundabout to join the A32 Gosport Road and head south into Gosport. Continue along the A32 as it becomes Fareham Road then, at the second roundabout in a junction with two roundabouts, take the 3rd exit (signposted Alverstoke, Stokes Bay, Privett Park) into Military Road. Continue straight down this road, pass the playing fields on the left, then turn left at the roundabout into Privett Road. The entrance to the ground is the 4th turning on the left, just after the junction with Privett Place.

HAVANT & WATERLOOVILLE FC

Founded: 1998
Former Names: Formed by the amalgamation of Waterlooville FC and Havant Town FC
Nickname: 'The Hawks'
Ground: Westleigh Park, Martin Road, Havant, PO9 5TH
Record Attendance: 5,757 (2006/07)
Pitch Size: 112 × 76 yards

Colours: White shirts with Blue Shoulders, White shorts
Telephone Nº: (023) 9278-7822 (Ground)
Fax Number: (023) 9226-2367
Ground Capacity: 5,250
Seating Capacity: 562
Web site: www.havantandwaterlooville.net

GENERAL INFORMATION

Car Parking: Space for 750 cars at the ground
Coach Parking: At the ground
Nearest Railway Station: Havant (1 mile)
Nearest Bus Station: Town Centre (1½ miles)
Club Shop: At the ground
Opening Times: Matchdays only
Telephone Nº: 07411 459350

GROUND INFORMATION

Away Supporters' Entrances & Sections:
Martin Road End

ADMISSION INFO (2013/2014 PRICES)

Adult Standing: £12.00
Adult Seating: £12.00
Senior Citizen Standing/Seating: £7.00
Concessionary Standing/Seating: £7.00
Note: When accompanied by a paying adult, children under the age of 11 are admitted free of charge

DISABLED INFORMATION

Wheelchairs: 12 spaces available in the Main Stand
Helpers: Admitted
Prices: Normal prices for disabled fans. Free for helpers
Disabled Toilets: Two available
Contact: (023) 9226-7276   (Bookings are necessary)

Travelling Supporters' Information:
Routes: From London or the North take the A27 from Chichester and exit at the B2149 turn-off for Havant. Take the 2nd exit off the dual carriageway into Bartons Road and then the 1st right into Martin Road for the ground; From the West: Take the M27 then the A27 to the Petersfield exit. Then as above.

HAYES & YEADING UNITED FC

No photograph of the Sharda Glass Community Stadium
was available at the time of going to print.

Hayes & Yeading United FC are groundsharing with Woking FC (see page 28 for details of Kingfield Stadium) during the first half of the 2013/2014 season. The club hopes to be able to move into their new ground at Beaconsfield Road, Hayes (which is still under construction) towards the end of 2013. Please contact the club for further details.

Founded: 2007
Former Names: Formed by the amalgamation of Hayes FC and Yeading FC in 2007
Nickname: 'United'
Ground: Sharda Glass Community Stadium, Beaconsfield Road, Hayes   UB4 0SL
Record Attendance: –
Pitch Size: 110 × 72 yards

Colours: Red Shirts with Black shorts
Telephone N°: (020) 8753-2075
Fax Number: (020) 8753-0933
Ground Capacity: 6,161
Seating Capacity: 2,511
Web site: www.hyufc.com

GENERAL INFORMATION
Car Parking: Limited number of spaces at the ground
Coach Parking: Contact the club for details
Nearest Railway Station: Hayes & Harlington or Southall (both approximately 2 miles)
Nearest Bus Station: –
Club Shop: None at present

GROUND INFORMATION
Away Supporters' Entrances & Sections:
Please contact the club for details.

ADMISSION INFO (2013/2014 PRICES)
Adult Standing: £12.00   **Adult Seating**: £12.00
Under-16s/Student Standing/Seating: £2.00
Senior Citizen Standing/Seating: £8.00

DISABLED INFORMATION
Wheelchairs: Please contact the club for further details
Helpers: Contact the club for details
Prices: Contact the club for details
Disabled Toilets: Available
Contact: (020) 8753-2075   (Bookings are necessary)

Travelling Supporters' Information:
Routes: Exit the M4 at Junction 4 and take the A312 northwards. Carry straight on at the first roundabout and cross the Grand Union Canal before passing Hayes & Harlington Station on the left. After approximately ½ mile, take the slip road off on the left and turn right at the roundabout (passing over the A312) into Uxbridge Road. Take the first turn on the right into the retail park (Springfield Road) and follow the road round left into Beaconsfield Road. The stadium is a short distance on the right.

MAIDENHEAD UNITED FC

Founded: 1870
Former Names: None
Nickname: 'Magpies'
Ground: York Road, Maidenhead, Berks. SL6 1SF
Record Attendance: 7,920 (1936)
Pitch Size: 110 × 75 yards

Colours: Black and White striped shirts, Black shorts
Telephone N°: (01628) 636314 (Club)
Contact Number: (01628) 636078
Ground Capacity: 4,500
Seating Capacity: 400
Web: www.pitchero.com/clubs/maidenheadunited/

GENERAL INFORMATION

Car Parking: Street parking
Coach Parking: Street parking
Nearest Railway Station: Maidenhead (¼ mile)
Nearest Bus Station: Maidenhead
Club Shop: At the ground
Opening Times: Matchdays only
Telephone N°: (01628) 624739

GROUND INFORMATION

Away Supporters' Entrances & Sections:
No usual segregation

ADMISSION INFO (2013/2014 PRICES)

Adult Standing: £10.00
Adult Seating: £10.00
Concessionary Standing and Seating: £6.00
Under-18s Standing and Seating: £2.00
Note: Junior Magpies (Under-16s) are admitted free

DISABLED INFORMATION

Wheelchairs: Accommodated
Helpers: Admitted
Prices: Normal prices for the disabled. Free for helpers
Disabled Toilets: Available
Contact: (01628) 636078   (Bookings are not necessary)

Travelling Supporters' Information:
Routes: Exit M4 at Junction 7 and take the A4 to Maidenhead. Cross the River Thames bridge and turn left at the 2nd roundabout passing through the traffic lights. York Road is first right and the ground is approximately 300 yards along on the left.

STAINES TOWN FC

Photograph courtesy of Laurence Wakefield

Founded: 1892
Former Names: Staines FC, Staines Vale FC, Staines Albany FC, Staines Projectile FC & Staines Lagonda FC
Nickname: 'The Swans'
Ground: Wheatsheaf Park, Wheatsheaf Lane, Staines TW18 2PD
Record Attendance: 2,860 (2007)
Pitch Size: 110 × 76 yards

Ground Capacity: 3,061
Seating Capacity: 500
Colours: Old Gold and Blue shirts with Blue shorts
Telephone Nº: 0782 506-7232
Office Address: 52 Station Road, Egham, Surrey, TW20 9LF
Web site: www.stainesmassive.co.uk

GENERAL INFORMATION

Car Parking: Large car park shared with The Thames Club
Coach Parking: At the ground
Nearest Railway Station: Staines (1 mile)
Nearest Bus Station: Staines Central (1 mile)
Club Shop: At the ground
Opening Times: Matchdays only
Telephone Nº: (01784) 463100

GROUND INFORMATION

Away Supporters' Entrances & Sections:
No usual segregation

ADMISSION INFO (2013/2014 PRICES)

Adult Standing: £12.00
Adult Seating: £12.00
Senior Citizen Standing/Seating: £6.00
Junior Standing/Seating: £5.00

DISABLED INFORMATION

Wheelchairs: Accommodated
Helpers: Admitted
Prices: Normal prices apply for the disabled. Free for helpers
Disabled Toilets: Available
Contact: (01784) 225943

Travelling Supporters' Information:
Routes: Exit the M25 at Junction 13 and take the A30 towards London. At the 'Crooked Billet' roundabout follow signs for Staines Town Centre. Pass under the bridge and bear left, passing the Elmsleigh Centre Car Parks and bear left at the next junction (opposite the Thames Lodge Hotel) into Laleham Road. Pass under the iron railway bridge by the river and continue along for ¾ mile. Turn right by the bollards into Wheatsheaf Lane and the ground is situated on the left by the Thames Club.

SUTTON UNITED FC

Founded: 1898
Former Names: Formed by the amalgamation of Sutton Guild Rovers FC and Sutton Association FC
Nickname: 'U's'
Ground: Borough Sports Ground, Gander Green Lane, Sutton, Surrey SM1 2EY
Record Attendance: 14,000 (1970)

Colours: Shirts are Amber with a Chocolate pin-stripe, Amber shorts
Telephone N°: (020) 8644-4440
Fax Number: (020) 8644-5120
Ground Capacity: 7,032
Seating Capacity: 765
Web site: www.suttonunited.net

GENERAL INFORMATION

Car Parking: 150 spaces behind the Main Stand
Coach Parking: Space for 1 coach in the car park
Nearest Railway Station: West Sutton (adjacent)
Club Shop: At the ground
Opening Times: Matchdays only
Telephone N°: (020) 8644-4440

GROUND INFORMATION

Away Supporters' Entrances & Sections:
Collingwood Road entrances and accommodation

ADMISSION INFO (2013/2014 PRICES)

Adult Standing: £12.00
Adult Seating: £13.00
Child Standing: £2.00
Child Seating: £3.00
Senior Citizen Standing: £6.00
Senior Citizen Seating: £7.00

DISABLED INFORMATION

Wheelchairs: 8 spaces are available under cover accommodated on the track perimeter
Helpers: Admitted
Prices: Normal prices apply
Disabled Toilets: Available alongside the Standing Terrace
Contact: (020) 8644-4440   (Bookings are necessary)

Travelling Supporters' Information:
Routes: Exit the M25 at Junction 8 (Reigate Hill) and travel North on the A217 for approximately 8 miles. Cross the A232 then turn right at the traffic lights (past Goose & Granit Public House) into Gander Green Lane. The ground is 300 yards on the left; From London: Gander Green Lane crosses the Sutton bypass 1 mile south of Rose Hill Roundabout. Avoid Sutton Town Centre, especially on Saturdays.

TONBRIDGE ANGELS FC

Founded: 1948
Former Names: Tonbridge FC
Nickname: 'The Angels'
Ground: Longmead Stadium, Darenth Avenue, Tonbridge TN10 3LW
Record Attendance: 2,411 (2011)

Colours: Blue and White shirts with Blue shorts
Telephone Nº: (01732) 352417
Ground Capacity: 3,014
Seating Capacity: 774
Web site: www.tonbridgeangelsonline.co.uk
E-mail: chcole1063@aol.com

GENERAL INFORMATION
Car Parking: At the ground
Coach Parking: At the ground
Nearest Railway Station: Tonbridge (2 miles)
Club Shop: At the ground
Opening Times: Matchdays only
Telephone Nº: (01732) 352417

GROUND INFORMATION
Away Supporters' Entrances & Sections:
No usual segregation

ADMISSION INFO (2013/2014 PRICES)
Adult Standing: £12.00
Adult Seating: £13.00
Student/Senior Citizen Standing: £6.00
Student/Senior Citizen Seating: £7.00
Under-12s Standing: £3.00
Under-12s Seating: £4.00
Note: Family Tickets are also available

DISABLED INFORMATION
Wheelchairs: Accommodated
Helpers: Admitted
Prices: Normal prices apply
Disabled Toilets: One available
Contact: (01732) 352417

Travelling Supporters' Information:
Routes: Take the A26 or A21 to Tonbridge Town Centre, pass through the High Street and head north up Shipbourne Road which is the A227 Gravesend road. Turn left at the 2nd mini-roundabout by the 'Pinnacles' Pub into Darenth Avenue. The ground is situated at the bottom end of Darenth Avenue.

WESTON-SUPER-MARE FC

Founded: 1899
Former Names: Christ Church Old Boys FC
Nickname: 'Seagulls'
Ground: Woodspring Stadium, Winterstoke Road, Weston-super-Mare   BS24 9AA
Record Attendance: 2,623 (vs Woking in F.A. Cup)
Pitch Size: 110 × 70 yards

Colours: White shirts with Black shorts
Telephone Nº: (01934) 621618
Fax Number: (01934) 622704
Ground Capacity: 3,071
Seating Capacity: 320
Web site: www.weston-s-mareafc.co.uk

GENERAL INFORMATION
Car Parking: 140 spaces available at the ground
Coach Parking: At the ground
Nearest Railway Station: Weston-super-Mare (1½ miles)
Nearest Bus Station: Weston-super-Mare (1½ miles)
Club Shop: At the ground
Opening Times: Matchdays only
Telephone Nº: (01934) 621618

GROUND INFORMATION
Away Supporters' Entrances & Sections:
No usual segregation

ADMISSION INFO (2013/2014 PRICES)
Adult Standing/Seating: £10.00
Senior Citizen Standing/Seating: £6.00
Under-16s Standing/Seating: £6.00
Note: Under-10s are admitted for £1.00 when accompanied by a paying adult or senior citizen

DISABLED INFORMATION
Wheelchairs: Accommodated in a special disabled section
Helpers: Admitted
Prices: Normal prices apply
Disabled Toilets: Two available
Contact: (01934) 621618   (Bookings are not necessary)

Travelling Supporters' Information:
Routes: Exit the M5 at Junction 21 and follow the dual carriageway (A370) to the 4th roundabout (Asda Winterstoke). Turn left, go over the mini-roundabout and continue for 800 yards. The ground is on the right.

WHITEHAWK FC

Founded: 1945
Former Names: Whitehawk & Manor Farm Old Boys
Nickname: 'The Hawks'
Ground: The Enclosed Ground, East Brighton Park, Brighton   BN2 5TS
Record Attendance: 2,100 (1988/89 season)

Colours: Red shirts and shorts
Telephone Nº: (01273) 609736
Ground Capacity: 3,000
Seating Capacity: 200
Web Site: www.whitehawkfc.co.uk

GENERAL INFORMATION

Car Parking: At the ground
Coach Parking: At the ground
Nearest Railway Station: London Road (3¼ miles)
Club Shop: None
Opening Times: –
Telephone Nº: –

GROUND INFORMATION

Away Supporters' Entrances & Sections:
No usual segregation

ADMISSION INFO (2013/2014 PRICES)

Adult Standing: £10.00
Adult Seating: £10.00
Concessionary Standing: £5.00
Concessionary Seating: £5.00

DISABLED INFORMATION

Wheelchairs: Accommodated
Helpers: Admitted
Prices: Concessionary prices are charged for the disabled and helpers
Disabled Toilets: None
Contact: (01273) 609736   (Bookings are not necessary)

Travelling Supporters' Information:
Routes: Take the M23/A23 to the junction with the A27 on the outskirts of Brighton then follow the A27 towards Lewes. After passing Sussex University on the left, take the slip road onto the B2123 (signposted Falmer, Rottingdean) and continue for approximately 2 miles before turning right at the traffic lights into Warren Road by the Downs Hotel. Continue for approximately 1 mile then turn left at the traffic lights into Wilson Avenue. After 1¼ miles, turn left at the foot of the hill into East Brighton Park.

Football Conference National 2012/2013 Season

	AFC Telford United	Alfreton Town	Barrow	Braintree Town	Cambridge United	Dartford	Ebbsfleet United	Forest Green Rovers	Gateshead	Grimsby Town	Hereford United	Hyde	Kidderminster Harriers	Lincoln City	Luton Town	Macclesfield Town	Mansfield Town	Newport County	Nuneaton Town	Southport	Stockport County	Tamworth	Woking	Wrexham
AFC Telford United		0-0	1-1	3-0	1-2	0-2	2-2	1-2	0-0	1-2	0-4	1-3	0-2	1-1	0-0	0-2	2-2	2-4	0-3	1-3	2-2	3-3	1-0	0-2
Alfreton Town	1-1		4-0	1-1	1-1	3-2	3-0	2-1	3-2	0-2	0-3	5-1	1-1	0-2	3-0	1-2	0-3	4-3	0-3	3-3	2-3	3-0	0-3	1-2
Barrow	0-0	1-3		0-1	1-4	0-0	1-1	2-2	0-2	2-2	0-2	1-1	1-1	1-2	1-0	1-0	0-4	0-3	1-2	3-2	0-2	2-0	2-0	0-1
Braintree Town	3-2	2-1	2-3		0-3	0-2	3-1	3-1	2-1	2-0	0-2	2-2	1-1	0-3	2-0	0-3	2-1	1-2	2-2	1-3	0-0	2-1	1-1	1-5
Cambridge United	3-3	0-3	2-1	1-0		1-2	1-1	0-0	3-0	0-0	1-3	0-1	1-3	2-1	2-2	2-0	4-1	0-0	1-3	2-0	4-1	1-1	1-0	1-4
Dartford	1-4	5-1	0-1	0-0	1-1		3-1	0-1	3-0	1-2	4-0	2-1	1-0	2-4	1-0	2-0	2-0	2-1	0-1	2-2	1-1	2-3	4-1	2-1
Ebbsfleet United	1-3	0-0	2-4	0-1	2-4	2-2		0-2	3-1	1-1	1-0	3-2	1-1	1-1	1-3	0-4	3-1	1-1	1-1	4-1	0-0	1-1	2-2	1-1
Forest Green Rovers	0-0	1-1	1-1	4-1	1-1	2-3	4-1		1-0	0-1	0-1	3-1	0-1	3-0	1-2	1-1	1-2	1-2	0-1	0-1	4-1	1-2	3-1	0-0
Gateshead	1-1	2-0	0-1	1-2	0-0	2-0	2-0	1-1		1-1	3-2	3-0	2-0	1-1	5-1	2-2	4-1	0-0	0-2	2-2	1-1	0-2	2-1	0-1
Grimsby Town	1-0	4-2	0-0	3-0	0-1	0-2	3-1	1-0	3-0		1-1	2-0	1-3	1-1	4-1	0-1	4-1	3-0	0-0	2-2	1-2	2-0	5-1	1-0
Hereford United	1-1	3-3	2-1	0-0	4-2	1-0	4-2	1-2	1-1	0-2		1-2	0-1	3-1	1-0	2-1	1-2	2-3	0-0	2-2	1-2	5-2	2-1	0-1
Hyde	2-1	1-1	0-0	1-2	2-1	3-0	1-0	0-1	1-1	3-2	5-2		0-4	1-5	1-2	1-1	0-1	0-1	2-2	0-2	0-1	2-1	7-0	2-0
Kidderminster Harriers	1-0	3-1	2-0	2-1	3-2	5-1	3-2	0-1	1-1	0-0	0-1	3-0		3-0	0-2	3-0	2-3	3-2	1-0	2-2	4-0	4-1	2-2	2-0
Lincoln City	3-2	1-2	0-0	3-0	0-0	2-1	1-1	1-2	1-1	1-4	3-2	3-2	1-0		1-2	2-3	0-1	2-4	2-1	1-0	3-3	2-1	0-2	1-2
Luton Town	0-1	3-0	6-1	2-3	3-2	0-2	2-0	1-1	2-2	1-1	1-1	1-2	1-2	3-0		4-1	2-3	2-2	2-0	3-1	1-0	0-0	3-1	0-0
Macclesfield Town	2-1	1-2	2-0	2-1	2-1	2-0	1-2	0-4	1-3	0-1	3-2	1-0	2-1	1-1			0-3	1-1	0-0	2-2	1-1	2-0	0-0	2-0
Mansfield Town	1-0	1-2	8-1	2-0	3-1	5-0	4-1	1-0	4-0	2-0	1-1	1-0	0-2	0-0	2-2	3-1		3-4	1-0	1-0	4-1	2-0	3-1	1-0
Newport County	2-1	2-0	0-2	1-0	6-2	0-0	1-0	0-5	3-1	0-0	2-0	1-3	1-2	2-1	5-2	4-1	2-0		4-0	2-1	0-0	2-2	2-3	1-1
Nuneaton Town	3-1	1-0	1-1	2-4	2-2	1-0	4-5	1-1	1-0	1-0	0-0	3-1	0-1	1-0	0-0	3-3	1-1	1-2		0-1	2-1	0-0	0-0	0-0
Southport	0-3	0-2	5-2	0-2	2-1	2-2	1-0	1-2	2-1	1-1	2-2	0-1	1-3	4-2	1-3	3-2	1-2	0-2	3-1		1-1	0-3	1-2	1-4
Stockport County	2-2	1-0	3-1	1-3	1-1	0-1	3-1	2-1	1-2	1-2	2-3	0-2	1-0	2-0	0-1	3-4	1-3	1-0	3-2	3-4		0-1	1-2	2-3
Tamworth	0-0	1-1	1-3	1-4	1-2	3-2	0-1	2-1	2-0	0-1	2-2	2-0	0-1	1-0	1-2	0-0	0-1	1-2	2-1	2-1	1-0		2-1	0-1
Woking	5-2	1-2	3-1	1-4	2-1	1-0	1-0	2-0	2-1	0-1	1-1	2-1	2-2	1-1	3-1	5-4	1-2	1-3	6-1	2-3	1-0	2-3		2-0
Wrexham	4-1	1-1	3-0	1-1	1-0	2-2	4-1	1-1	1-1	0-0	1-2	2-0	1-2	2-4	0-0	0-0	2-1	2-0	6-1	2-2	3-1	2-2	3-1	

Football Conference National

Season 2012/2013

Team							
Mansfield Town	46	30	5	11	92	52	95
Kidderminster Harriers	46	28	9	9	82	40	93
Newport County	46	25	10	11	85	60	85
Grimsby Town	46	23	14	9	70	38	83
Wrexham	46	22	14	10	74	45	80
Hereford United	46	19	13	14	73	63	70
Luton Town	46	18	13	15	70	62	67
Dartford	46	19	9	18	67	63	66
Braintree Town	46	19	9	18	63	72	66
Forest Green Rovers	46	18	11	17	63	49	65
Macclesfield Town	46	17	12	17	65	70	63
Woking	46	18	8	20	73	81	62
Alfreton Town	46	16	12	18	69	74	60
Cambridge United	46	15	14	17	68	69	59
Nuneaton Town	46	14	15	17	55	63	57
Lincoln City	46	15	11	20	66	73	56
Gateshead	46	13	16	17	58	61	55
Hyde	46	16	7	23	63	75	55
Tamworth	46	15	10	21	55	69	55
Southport	46	14	12	20	72	86	54
Stockport County	46	13	11	22	57	80	50
Barrow	46	11	13	22	45	83	46
Ebbsfleet United	46	8	15	23	55	89	39
AFC Telford United	46	6	17	23	52	79	35

Promotion Play-offs

Wrexham .... 1 Kidderminster Harriers 0
Grimsby Town .... 0 Newport County 1

Kidderminster Harriers .... 1 Wrexham 3
Wrexham won 4-1 on aggregate
Newport County .... 1 Grimsby Town 0
Newport County won 2-0 on aggregate

Wrexham .... 0 Newport County 2

Promoted: Mansfield Town and Newport County

Relegated: Stockport County, Barrow, Ebbsfleet United and AFC Telford United

Football Conference North 2012/2013 Season	Altrincham	Bishop's Stortford	Boston United	Brackley Town	Bradford Park Avenue	Chester	Colwyn Bay	Corby Town	Droylsden	FC Halifax Town	Gainsborough Trinity	Gloucester City	Guiseley	Harrogate Town	Hinckley United	Histon	Oxford City	Solihull Moors	Stalybridge Celtic	Vauxhall Motors	Worcester City	Workington
Altrincham		2-1	7-1	1-4	3-1	2-4	1-1	2-1	6-0	2-0	0-1	2-0	1-3	3-0	8-0	5-0	3-1	2-1	2-1	1-0	2-0	1-2
Bishop's Stortford	1-1		1-0	1-3	2-1	1-2	2-2	2-1	2-1	1-2	1-5	1-2	2-5	0-2	1-1	3-1	0-0	4-1	0-0	2-2	0-1	0-3
Boston United	2-3	1-1		3-4	0-4	3-2	1-0	1-1	5-1	1-2	2-1	4-0	1-3	1-2	1-2	6-0	3-1	2-2	2-2	0-1	1-2	1-3
Brackley Town	0-1	1-0	0-2		3-1	2-3	1-3	2-4	3-2	0-0	2-2	0-1	1-0	2-1	5-0	2-1	0-0	2-1	4-1	1-0	2-0	3-1
Bradford Park Avenue	2-2	2-1	2-1	0-1		0-0	1-2	2-0	5-0	1-1	0-2	2-1	1-3	1-0	4-0	0-0	1-2	1-0	1-3	2-0	2-2	1-0
Chester	2-0	4-1	1-0	0-0	1-1		2-1	2-1	5-0	2-1	3-1	2-0	4-0	2-0	3-0	2-1	2-0	0-1	4-1	2-0	4-2	1-0
Colwyn Bay	1-3	1-2	0-2	1-1	1-2	1-5		1-0	1-3	0-3	1-0	1-0	0-2	1-2	3-2	3-1	3-1	3-1	2-3	2-4	0-3	1-4
Corby Town	2-5	2-2	2-1	0-4	4-5	1-2	3-1		5-0	1-5	0-0	3-2	2-3	0-2	5-3	0-0	1-1	2-3	1-0	0-1	1-0	1-3
Droylsden	0-5	1-2	0-1	0-3	0-7	3-4	2-0	2-2		0-6	1-3	1-0	0-3	1-3	3-2	2-2	1-3	2-4	1-1	5-2	0-2	0-1
FC Halifax Town	3-4	1-1	1-2	0-0	0-1	1-1	0-1	2-0	4-1		3-1	5-0	1-1	1-2	7-0	3-3	3-1	0-0	0-0	4-0	5-0	5-1
Gainsborough Trinity	2-4	2-2	2-2	0-1	1-1	0-2	3-1	2-2	3-0	3-0		0-1	1-2	1-1	5-0	1-0	1-2	1-1	1-2	2-1	1-0	1-1
Gloucester City	0-0	5-1	1-0	1-4	1-0	0-1	2-2	0-1	4-0	1-2	1-2		2-2	0-2	4-1	1-1	0-1	1-1	4-3	1-1	4-2	0-1
Guiseley	1-1	1-2	2-1	0-2	1-0	2-1	2-2	2-1	7-1	1-1	2-0	3-1		2-0	2-4	2-1	1-0	1-0	1-0	2-1	3-3	2-0
Harrogate Town	1-2	2-2	4-2	6-1	1-1	1-3	1-2	6-1	1-1	1-1	0-0	1-0	1-2		5-0	2-0	1-3	2-4	0-0	3-1	3-1	3-1
Hinckley United	0-6	1-5	2-4	1-3	1-4	0-6	1-3	6-3	2-2	0-2	0-2	0-3	0-3	0-2		0-1	0-2	1-1	0-3	0-6	0-5	1-1
Histon	2-0	2-0	1-1	3-0	1-4	1-4	2-1	3-4	3-1	0-1	0-3	2-1	1-4	1-3	2-1		1-1	0-0	0-2	2-0	0-0	3-0
Oxford City	2-2	1-1	4-2	2-1	1-1	0-1	1-2	2-0	2-2	2-2	1-1	2-1	0-3	0-0	6-2	0-0		1-2	0-0	1-1	2-2	5-0
Solihull Moors	2-1	0-1	1-0	0-1	3-1	0-3	2-0	3-0	2-1	0-3	0-2	2-3	2-0	2-0	1-0	1-1	1-2		1-0	2-3	0-1	2-2
Stalybridge Celtic	2-2	3-1	0-1	0-3	2-0	2-6	3-3	1-2	0-0	1-0	1-1	4-0	1-1	1-0	4-0	2-1	2-2	0-3		0-1	0-2	1-4
Vauxhall Motors	2-1	2-2	4-0	0-2	1-3	0-3	1-1	1-1	4-0	1-3	1-2	1-2	2-0	0-1	2-1	2-0	2-1	2-1	0-0		1-0	1-3
Worcester City	0-0	2-0	0-3	1-2	2-0	0-1	2-0	5-1	2-1	0-1	0-3	0-1	0-1	2-2	3-1	2-3	3-2	1-3	1-2	2-2		1-1
Workington	2-1	2-3	1-1	0-0	1-6	1-1	1-2	2-3	2-1	0-1	0-3	0-1	0-2	1-2	2-1	3-1	1-2	1-1	4-1	3-1	1-0	

Football Conference North

Season 2012/2013

Chester	42	34	5	3	103	32	107
Guiseley	42	28	7	7	83	45	91
Brackley Town	42	26	7	9	76	44	85
Altrincham	42	24	8	10	100	51	80
FC Halifax Town	42	21	9	12	86	38	75
Harrogate Town	42	20	9	13	72	50	69
Bradford Park Avenue	42	19	9	14	75	52	66
Gainsborough Trinity	42	18	12	12	68	45	66
Solihull Moors	42	17	9	16	57	53	60
Oxford City	42	13	16	13	62	57	55
Gloucester City	42	16	6	20	54	63	54
Vauxhall Motors	42	15	8	19	58	64	53
Stalybridge Celtic	42	13	13	16	55	62	52
Workington	42	16	8	18	60	68	52
Worcester City	42	14	8	20	57	62	50
Boston United	42	14	7	21	68	73	49
Bishop's Stortford	42	12	13	17	58	74	49
Colwyn Bay	42	14	7	21	57	78	49
Histon	42	11	11	20	48	73	44
Corby Town	42	12	8	22	66	92	44
Droylsden	42	5	7	30	43	124	22
Hinckley United	42	3	4	35	37	143	7

Workington had 4 points deducted for fielding an ineligible player.

Hinckley United had 3 points deducted for failing to pay football creditors then a further 3 points deducted for failing to fulfil their fixture against Bishop's Stortford.

Promotion Play-offs North

Altrincham 2   Brackley Town 1
FC Halifax Town 1   Guiseley 1

Guiseley 0   FC Halifax Town 2
FC Halifax Town won 3-1 on aggregate
Brackley Town 3   Altrincham 0
Brackley Town won 4-2 on aggregate

Brackley Town 0   FC Halifax Town 1

Promoted: Chester and FC Halifax Town
Relegated: Corby Town, Droylsden and Hinckley United

Football Conference South
2012/2013 Season

	AFC Hornchurch	Basingstoke Town	Bath City	Billericay Town	Boreham Wood	Bromley	Chelmsford City	Dorchester Town	Dover Athletic	Eastbourne Borough	Eastleigh	Farnborough	Havant & Waterlooville	Hayes & Yeading United	Maidenhead United	Salisbury City	Staines Town	Sutton United	Tonbridge Angels	Truro City	Welling United	Weston-super-Mare
AFC Hornchurch		3-0	2-1	1-0	1-1	1-0	0-2	1-0	0-1	0-1	1-0	1-1	2-2	2-0	0-2	2-2	1-1	1-1	1-1	1-2	0-3	0-0
Basingstoke Town	0-2		2-1	3-3	2-3	1-1	1-2	2-1	0-1	2-2	0-3	6-2	1-2	2-2	2-0	0-4	3-1	2-1	1-0	3-2	0-1	1-3
Bath City	3-1	1-1		2-1	0-0	0-2	2-2	2-3	1-2	2-2	1-1	3-2	2-0	2-3	3-1	0-0	0-1	0-4	3-0	1-1	1-0	1-2
Billericay Town	1-1	1-3	2-0		1-1	2-3	0-1	3-1	1-2	1-2	4-0	2-1	3-1	4-1	1-0	1-2	2-3	2-4	3-3	2-1	1-2	0-0
Boreham Wood	2-1	1-1	0-0	3-0		1-2	0-0	1-2	1-1	2-1	3-0	3-1	1-2	3-0	2-1	1-0	1-1	3-0	4-2	0-0	1-1	0-1
Bromley	4-0	1-2	1-0	0-1	1-1		2-0	2-1	0-4	0-2	3-1	1-3	1-1	0-4	3-2	1-2	0-0	0-2	1-1	4-0	0-2	0-1
Chelmsford City	1-4	2-0	0-1	1-1	2-1	3-2		4-0	0-3	1-0	1-1	6-0	1-1	6-2	3-1	2-1	3-2	1-0	2-1	3-2	2-3	2-1
Dorchester Town	3-1	2-2	2-1	6-1	0-0	0-4	1-0		1-0	2-1	1-0	2-0	0-0	2-2	4-0	2-1	0-4	0-1	1-2	2-2	2-1	2-1
Dover Athletic	1-0	0-5	2-0	4-1	0-1	1-0	0-1	0-0		0-0	2-0	2-2	2-2	2-1	2-0	1-3	0-1	1-1	0-1	3-2	3-2	3-1
Eastbourne Borough	1-1	1-0	0-3	2-1	1-1	3-0	1-2	0-0	0-3		1-0	0-1	0-1	2-1	0-2	1-2	2-0	0-1	1-2	1-0	0-3	0-2
Eastleigh	1-0	1-1	3-1	5-0	1-1	3-0	1-0	3-1	1-3	1-0		3-1	2-2	3-1	4-2	1-0	4-3	1-0	4-1	3-1	1-3	3-0
Farnborough	1-1	2-1	0-1	4-3	0-3	2-0	3-1	1-1	5-2	0-1	6-2		1-1	4-1	2-1	2-1	3-1	1-3	4-1	4-1	0-3	2-1
Havant & Waterlooville	5-2	4-1	2-1	5-0	1-1	1-2	1-1	4-0	1-1	2-3	0-3	0-1		2-1	2-1	2-2	3-1	3-0	2-2	1-0	0-1	0-3
Hayes & Yeading United	1-3	2-1	2-2	4-2	0-1	1-1	3-0	1-3	2-4	1-1	2-1	3-2	1-4		1-1	2-3	4-0	0-0	3-2	1-2	2-1	2-1
Maidenhead United	2-4	2-2	0-1	3-2	2-1	4-2	2-1	1-2	1-2	1-2	0-2	3-2	2-0	0-2		0-1	1-1	0-1	3-1	8-0	2-1	0-1
Salisbury City	2-1	0-2	3-2	2-0	2-2	3-1	3-2	4-0	1-1	1-0	5-3	1-0	5-1	2-0	1-1		3-1	1-0	2-0	4-3	2-1	1-1
Staines Town	3-1	2-0	1-3	1-2	1-1	3-1	1-3	2-1	0-2	0-2	1-3	1-2	1-1	7-1	0-6	3-2		1-4	1-4	1-0	2-2	1-1
Sutton United	3-1	3-2	0-2	3-0	2-1	4-3	1-0	1-2	2-2	2-0	2-1	0-1	1-1	5-1	1-1	1-0	1-2		2-2	0-1	2-1	1-3
Tonbridge Angels	1-0	0-0	3-4	1-1	4-2	0-3	0-4	0-2	2-1	1-1	3-1	2-3	1-0	1-1	2-1	1-2	1-0	1-1		3-2	1-1	1-1
Truro City	3-2	2-2	2-1	2-4	2-0	0-1	1-2	1-2	0-3	2-2	1-3	3-3	3-3	3-1	0-1	1-1	0-3	1-2	2-0		0-3	1-2
Welling United	4-0	1-1	1-1	5-2	4-0	3-1	3-0	3-2	1-1	2-0	1-1	2-0	1-0	3-0	3-2	1-0	3-2	2-2	4-1	4-3		4-1
Weston-super-Mare	1-0	5-2	1-4	1-0	2-4	3-0	3-0	2-0	0-3	3-2	2-4	1-1	2-2	1-1	0-3	1-0	1-1	2-0	0-2	2-0	2-0	

Football Conference South
Season 2012/2013

Welling United	42	26	8	8	90	44	86
Salisbury City	42	25	8	9	80	47	82
Dover Athletic	42	22	10	10	69	44	76
Eastleigh	42	22	6	14	79	61	72
Chelmsford City	42	22	6	14	70	56	72
Sutton United	42	20	10	12	66	49	70
Weston-super-Mare	42	19	10	13	61	55	67
Dorchester Town	42	19	8	15	59	62	65
Boreham Wood	42	15	17	10	59	46	62
Havant & Waterlooville	42	14	16	12	68	60	58
Bath City	42	15	10	17	60	58	55
Eastbourne Borough	42	14	9	19	42	52	51
Farnborough	42	19	7	16	76	75	50
Basingstoke Town	42	12	12	18	63	73	48
Bromley	42	14	6	22	54	69	48
Tonbridge Angels	42	12	12	18	56	77	48
Hayes & Yeading United	42	13	9	20	64	89	48
Staines Town	42	13	8	21	61	78	47
Maidenhead United	42	13	6	23	64	68	45
AFC Hornchurch	42	11	11	20	47	64	44
Billericay Town	42	11	7	24	62	90	40
Truro City	42	9	8	25	57	90	25

Truro had 10 points deducted for entering administration.
Farnborough had 4 points deducted for fielding an ineligible player then a further 10 points deducted for entering administration.
Salisbury City had 1 point deducted for fielding an ineligible player.

Promotion Play-offs South

Chelmsford City	1	Salisbury City	0
Eastleigh	1	Dover Athletic	3

Salisbury City	2	Chelmsford City	0

Salisbury City won 2-1 on aggregate

Dover Athletic	0	Eastleigh	2 (aet)

Aggregate 3-3. Dover Athletic won 4-2 on penalties

Salisbury City	3	Dover Athletic	2 (aet)

Promoted: Welling United and Salisbury City

Relegated: AFC Hornchurch, Billericay Town and Truro City

The Evo-Stik League Northern Premier League Premier Division 2012/2013 Season	AFC Fylde	Ashton United	Blyth Spartans	Buxton	Chorley	Eastwood Town	FC United of Manchester	Frickley Athletic	Grantham Town	Hednesford Town	Ilkeston	Kendal Town	Marine	Matlock Town	Nantwich Town	North Ferriby United	Rushall Olympic	Stafford Rangers	Stocksbridge Park Steels	Whitby Town	Witton Albion	Worksop Town
AFC Fylde		1-2	1-0	5-0	0-1	5-1	4-2	3-2	5-3	1-2	2-3	4-0	2-0	3-0	3-2	1-0	1-3	0-1	4-0	4-3	1-2	2-2
Ashton United	2-2		2-0	0-1	3-2	6-0	1-2	0-0	1-1	2-2	0-3	4-1	2-4	2-0	2-1	0-2	2-3	0-0	2-3	2-2	1-3	5-3
Blyth Spartans	0-5	4-1		2-2	1-3	1-0	1-2	4-2	1-0	1-2	3-2	1-3	3-3	2-1	1-1	0-1	1-1	1-0	5-0	2-2	0-3	3-2
Buxton	1-0	6-1	2-0		1-1	6-2	0-3	1-0	1-1	0-2	0-0	1-2	1-4	1-0	3-1	2-0	2-0	2-1	7-0	2-1	2-2	0-3
Chorley	1-4	1-1	1-0	2-1		1-1	1-2	5-1	2-0	1-2	1-0	5-0	1-0	1-0	3-3	0-1	1-6	2-0	1-1	2-3	1-2	1-1
Eastwood Town	1-4	0-5	1-4	1-5	0-1		2-2	0-1	2-2	0-2	1-4	2-5	1-2	3-3	1-5	0-5	2-1	2-2	1-2	0-2	3-4	0-1
FC United of Manchester	2-1	3-0	2-1	1-2	1-3	4-1		3-0	1-0	1-1	1-0	6-0	0-1	4-0	1-2	1-1	0-4	3-0	4-0	3-2	0-1	1-0
Frickley Athletic	1-1	1-1	2-1	3-3	0-1	1-0	2-4		0-0	2-1	2-1	2-1	0-2	1-2	3-0	2-3	3-3	2-1	4-2	0-2	0-2	0-0
Grantham Town	1-2	0-2	2-2	0-0	0-1	4-0	2-4	2-1		2-3	1-1	3-4	1-0	3-3	1-4	2-3	2-1	2-2	1-2	2-3	1-3	3-0
Hednesford Town	2-0	1-2	3-0	3-2	3-1	2-0	1-0	3-2	3-0		2-0	2-1	2-0	2-2	3-0	2-3	3-4	2-2	4-1	4-0	2-1	0-4
Ilkeston	1-1	2-2	3-1	1-1	1-0	2-1	1-1	4-2	2-0	0-2		4-4	1-0	0-2	3-0	2-2	0-1	0-2	1-0	3-1	2-3	2-1
Kendal Town	2-2	2-2	1-3	1-0	1-4	6-0	1-5	0-2	1-0	1-3	3-2		2-3	4-1	0-1	2-4	0-2	2-2	0-5	2-4	1-2	3-4
Marine	0-4	0-0	5-1	2-0	2-0	2-0	0-3	2-2	1-0	0-0	1-1	2-2		1-3	2-1	1-3	1-1	3-1	2-1	2-5	3-0	2-3
Matlock Town	2-1	2-2	1-3	1-1	1-0	0-1	2-2	3-1	3-2	2-3	1-1	3-0	1-0		0-5	0-2	0-3	2-3	1-1	0-0	1-2	1-5
Nantwich Town	0-3	0-2	2-1	2-2	0-1	1-0	2-3	3-2	0-2	1-1	1-0	1-1	2-3	0-1		2-3	0-2	1-1	4-3	2-1	2-1	0-5
North Ferriby United	0-1	2-0	3-2	1-1	1-0	6-1	1-1	4-0	3-1	2-3	1-1	3-2	3-1	2-1	0-0		2-2	1-1	5-1	1-1	2-0	2-0
Rushall Olympic	2-0	0-0	5-2	0-1	0-0	2-0	0-1	1-0	3-1	2-2	2-1	1-0	2-0	0-4	2-3	0-3		1-1	1-1	1-1	0-4	0-1
Stafford Rangers	4-2	0-0	2-4	2-2	1-0	2-0	1-1	3-3	0-1	0-1	2-1	5-1	0-0	1-0	2-0	0-2	1-2		1-1	0-1	0-0	3-1
Stocksbridge Park Steels	0-2	0-3	2-3	0-2	4-5	1-1	1-3	4-3	0-3	3-3	1-1	5-3	2-2	2-3	5-2	0-4	3-0	2-0		1-4	3-3	1-2
Whitby Town	0-4	1-3	1-3	1-1	1-1	1-1	0-1	4-1	2-0	0-2	0-4	1-0	1-1	1-0	1-2	2-4	0-1	4-0	3-2		1-3	2-2
Witton Albion	0-2	0-2	2-1	2-4	1-3	3-0	1-1	5-0	0-2	1-1	2-2	3-0	2-0	3-0	2-2	2-4	2-0	3-1	1-0	4-2		4-3
Worksop Town	0-0	5-1	8-1	2-0	1-0	2-3	4-1	3-2	3-2	0-4	1-4	3-0	1-1	6-1	0-2	2-1	2-3	2-3	2-1	0-1	1-1	

Evo-Stik League (Northern) Premier Division

Season 2012/2013

Team	P	W	D	L	F	A	Pts
North Ferriby United	42	28	9	5	96	43	93
Hednesford Town	42	28	9	5	91	47	93
FC United of Manchester	42	25	8	9	86	48	83
Witton Albion	42	24	8	10	85	57	80
AFC Fylde	42	23	6	13	93	51	75
Rushall Olympic	42	20	10	12	69	55	70
Buxton	42	18	13	11	72	56	67
Chorley	42	20	7	15	63	52	67
Worksop Town	42	20	6	16	91	68	66
Ashton United	42	15	14	13	71	66	59
Marine	42	16	11	15	61	61	59
Ilkeston	42	15	13	14	67	55	58
Whitby Town	42	16	9	17	68	72	57
Nantwich Town	42	15	8	19	63	76	53
Stafford Rangers	42	12	15	15	54	60	51
Blyth Spartans	42	15	6	21	70	87	51
Matlock Town	42	12	9	21	54	80	45
Frickley Athletic	42	10	9	23	58	88	39
Grantham Town	42	9	9	24	56	75	36
Stocksbridge Park Steels	42	9	9	24	67	106	36
Kendal Town	42	9	6	27	65	112	33
Eastwood Town	42	3	6	33	36	121	15

Promotion Play-offs

Hednesford Town 3   AFC Fylde .... 3 (aet)
Hednesford Town won 3-1 on penalties
FC United of Manchester 3   Witton Albion 1

Hednesford Town 2   FC United of Manchester 1

Promoted: North Ferriby United and Hednesford Town
Relegated: Kendal Town and Eastwood Town

The Evo-stik League Southern Premier Division 2012/2013 Season	AFC Totton	Arlesey Town	Banbury United	Barwell	Bashley	Bedford Town	Bedworth United	Bideford	Cambridge City	Chesham United	Chippenham Town	Frome Town	Gosport Borough	Hemel Hempstead Town	Kettering Town	Hitchin Town	Leamington	Redditch United	St. Albans City	St. Neots Town	Stourbridge	Weymouth
AFC Totton		3-3	2-3	2-1	2-0	2-0	3-2	2-0	1-5	1-1	0-5	2-0	3-2	2-0	4-0	2-2	0-2	2-0	3-0	2-1	2-4	5-2
Arlesey Town	5-0		2-1	0-1	1-2	2-1	1-0	2-2	1-2	2-0	4-0	0-1	1-1	3-1	3-0	3-1	0-2	3-0	1-3	4-3	2-4	3-0
Banbury United	2-1	1-3		1-2	3-1	1-1	1-1	1-1	2-2	1-2	1-0	1-1	2-4	4-0	2-0	0-4	3-0	0-0	2-2	3-1	0-2	1-3
Barwell	1-0	2-0	4-1		0-0	2-1	2-0	1-1	1-0	1-3	0-0	1-1	1-2	2-2	1-2	1-0	1-3	0-0	1-3	2-3	2-1	0-1
Bashley	0-3	1-0	2-0	0-5		0-1	1-0	4-1	0-0	1-3	2-1	2-1	1-1	0-6	3-1	0-1	0-2	0-1	2-0	2-2	0-1	1-0
Bedford Town	4-1	0-0	3-1	3-0	0-1		0-1	3-1	2-1	0-1	1-1	0-1	1-0	0-3	1-1	1-4	2-2	2-1	2-0	3-0	2-0	0-2
Bedworth United	2-0	2-1	0-4	1-1	0-3	2-0		2-1	0-2	1-1	2-2	1-0	1-1	1-2	0-1	1-0	0-3	0-1	1-3	1-3	0-3	2-0
Bideford	1-1	1-1	1-2	1-2	0-0	0-3	3-0		2-1	2-1	1-2	0-0	0-2	3-2	4-0	3-2	0-1	3-2	1-0	0-0	2-2	2-1
Cambridge City	0-0	1-2	1-0	2-1	3-1	2-1	3-0	1-0		1-0	2-3	1-2	0-4	0-1	1-1	0-0	1-4	1-0	2-1	0-5	2-2	1-0
Chesham United	6-0	1-0	3-1	2-2	3-0	2-2	3-0	1-0	1-0		1-1	1-1	0-3	0-0	0-0	1-1	1-1	2-1	2-1	2-1	1-1	1-2
Chippenham Town	3-0	0-0	0-2	1-1	1-0	0-2	1-1	1-7	4-3	2-3		2-2	0-0	1-2	3-0	2-4	0-2	2-3	4-3	2-2	4-0	2-2
Frome Town	3-1	0-1	0-0	2-3	1-1	2-3	1-3	0-1	0-3	0-0	2-0		1-1	1-3	3-1	2-1	0-2	1-0	0-3	1-2	0-1	2-0
Gosport Borough	1-0	0-1	3-2	1-2	0-0	4-0	1-0	2-0	1-2	3-1	2-3	0-0		3-3	7-0	0-0	3-0	2-3	0-1	1-0	1-3	0-0
Hemel Hempstead Town	4-1	1-2	1-2	1-1	4-2	4-3	6-1	4-1	1-0	1-2	2-1	0-3	1-1		5-2	8-2	1-3	4-0	1-1	2-4	2-1	1-3
Kettering Town	1-1	1-3	1-1	1-2	0-7	3-0	1-4	3-1	1-2	3-1	2-4	1-1	1-3	1-2		3-1	1-3	0-1	2-6	1-0	0-1	1-6
Hitchin Town	4-0	0-1	1-2	0-1	3-2	2-0	1-1	1-0	0-3	1-3	2-1	2-0	1-0	3-2	3-4		0-1	3-0	0-2	2-2	0-1	1-2
Leamington	2-1	4-3	4-1	0-6	4-1	3-0	6-1	2-1	1-0	0-1	1-0	2-0	1-3	3-2	2-1	3-0		2-0	2-1	3-0	1-1	1-1
Redditch United	2-1	0-2	0-2	0-1	0-0	0-3	0-0	2-1	2-4	0-2	1-0	2-1	0-2	1-4	4-1	0-2	1-1		0-2	1-0	0-4	0-0
St. Albans City	3-0	1-0	4-0	4-4	2-2	2-2	3-0	4-3	3-2	2-6	0-2	4-0	1-6	0-1	2-1	1-1	3-0	3-0		0-1	2-4	2-3
St. Neots Town	1-3	1-2	3-2	2-2	2-2	1-3	3-2	5-3	2-3	3-1	0-1	0-1	2-3	6-1	4-3	2-3	0-1	1-2	3-2		0-0	4-2
Stourbridge	3-0	4-1	8-1	0-2	3-0	0-1	0-1	3-1	4-1	5-0	2-1	1-1	1-1	2-3	0-0	4-1	5-1	1-0	2-1	0-1		5-0
Weymouth	3-3	2-1	1-0	2-1	1-0	0-4	2-1	4-2	0-1	0-3	0-0	2-1	3-3	0-1	0-0	3-2	0-4	0-2	2-0	3-1	1-5	

The Evo-Stik League Southern
Premier Division

Season 2012/2013

Leamington	42	30	5	7	85	46	95	
Stourbridge	42	25	8	9	94	42	83	
Chesham United	42	21	12	9	69	48	75	
Hemel Hempstead Town	42	22	6	14	95	71	72	
Gosport Borough	42	19	13	10	78	43	70	
Arlesey Town	42	21	6	15	70	51	69	
Barwell	42	19	12	11	67	50	69	
Cambridge City	42	20	6	16	63	57	66	
Weymouth	42	18	8	16	59	71	62	
Bedford Town	42	18	7	17	61	56	61	
St Albans City	42	18	6	18	81	71	60	
St Neots Town	42	15	7	20	77	77	52	
Hitchin Town	42	15	7	20	62	68	52	
AFC Totton	42	15	7	20	62	84	52	
Chippenham Town	42	13	12	17	63	67	51	
Banbury United	42	14	9	19	60	75	51	
Bashley	42	13	10	19	47	63	49	
Frome Town	42	11	12	19	40	55	45	
Redditch United	42	12	7	23	32	65	43	
Bideford	42	11	9	22	58	73	42	
Bedworth United	42	11	9	22	39	73	42	
Kettering Town	42	8	8	26	47	102	22	

Kettering Town had 10 points deducted for financial irregularities.

Promotion Play-offs

Stourbridge 1   Gosport Borough 2
Chesham United 0   Hemel Hempstead Town 2

Hemel Hempstead Town 2   Gosport Borough .... 2 (aet)
Gosport Borough won 5-4 on penalties.

Promoted: Leamington and Gosport Borough

Relegated: Bedworth United and Kettering Town

Ryman Football League Premier Division 2012/2013 Season	Bognor Regis Town	Bury Town	Canvey Island	Carshalton Athletic	Concord Rangers	Cray Wanderers	East Thurrock United	Enfield Town	Hampton & Richmond Borough	Harrow Borough	Hastings United	Hendon	Kingstonian	Leiston	Lewes	Lowestoft Town	Margate	Metropolitan Police	Thurrock	Wealdstone	Whitehawk	Wingate & Finchley
Bognor Regis Town	■	5-1	2-2	2-1	0-1	0-2	1-0	0-0	0-5	0-3	1-0	3-1	0-1	1-1	3-1	0-2	0-2	0-0	1-0	0-1	1-3	1-0
Bury Town	2-0	■	1-0	1-1	0-4	0-2	1-2	2-1	0-1	0-1	1-0	1-2	1-0	3-3	2-1	1-1	2-2	0-2	3-1	0-0	1-3	4-2
Canvey Island	1-1	0-1	■	4-2	0-2	1-0	2-1	3-4	0-0	3-0	1-1	0-3	4-3	2-0	0-0	0-2	3-1	0-1	2-0	2-0	1-2	3-2
Carshalton Athletic	0-2	1-3	0-2	■	1-2	2-1	1-1	3-2	3-0	3-1	1-0	1-2	1-3	1-3	3-3	2-0	4-0	1-1	0-1	0-2	0-1	1-2
Concord Rangers	1-3	3-2	3-0	6-3	■	0-4	2-2	3-0	2-1	1-2	4-0	1-2	0-3	0-0	3-6	1-1	2-1	5-1	1-1	2-2	2-2	4-1
Cray Wanderers	1-3	2-2	1-1	3-2	0-2	■	2-2	1-5	2-0	2-1	0-3	0-1	1-3	0-0	2-2	1-1	0-4	1-2	0-0	0-3	1-2	3-4
East Thurrock United	4-4	1-3	2-0	4-0	3-1	1-1	■	2-0	1-2	2-0	1-0	2-0	1-1	2-2	1-0	0-2	0-0	2-2	1-0	0-2	1-1	2-0
Enfield Town	0-1	2-3	0-2	1-2	0-1	1-3	2-3	■	0-2	2-0	1-0	6-3	1-1	1-0	2-1	2-3	0-3	4-0	1-1	1-2	1-3	2-1
Hampton & Richmond Borough	1-0	2-3	2-2	0-1	1-1	1-3	0-3	4-2	■	0-0	1-0	1-2	1-0	3-3	2-1	1-1	1-2	0-0	1-0	3-1	1-0	3-3
Harrow Borough	3-2	3-1	1-3	1-0	1-2	3-3	2-3	4-2	4-3	■	0-1	1-1	1-0	1-3	0-2	3-3	0-2	2-3	4-1	0-0	3-1	1-2
Hastings United	1-1	0-1	0-0	1-4	2-2	1-1	1-1	3-2	0-0	2-0	■	1-2	1-0	0-1	3-3	1-4	2-2	1-2	1-1	1-1	0-2	2-1
Hendon	1-0	2-2	1-2	3-1	2-2	0-0	0-0	2-3	0-3	1-2	2-0	■	1-0	2-1	2-2	0-1	0-0	1-1	1-0	0-0	1-1	0-2
Kingstonian	1-0	0-2	1-2	2-1	0-1	9-3	0-2	1-2	0-0	4-2	0-1	2-1	■	3-1	3-1	0-1	3-3	1-0	1-0	2-0	2-3	0-1
Leiston	1-1	0-0	1-1	1-0	0-3	1-1	5-4	3-1	2-2	1-0	3-1	0-1	2-2	■	1-1	0-0	1-2	0-2	2-1	1-1	0-2	3-0
Lewes	1-0	2-3	1-2	2-1	0-3	2-2	1-1	1-2	2-2	1-1	1-2	0-0	1-2	0-1	■	2-1	2-0	1-2	1-2	1-0	2-3	3-1
Lowestoft Town	1-2	1-0	2-0	2-3	4-1	4-1	0-0	0-0	5-3	3-0	1-0	1-3	1-1	2-0	2-0	■	1-0	2-1	0-1	3-0	0-0	3-0
Margate	3-0	3-1	2-2	3-1	0-2	0-1	0-1	2-0	2-1	2-1	0-1	1-2	0-2	1-2	2-0	1-1	■	1-2	3-1	2-4	2-1	2-0
Metropolitan Police	3-2	3-1	2-1	1-0	0-2	2-4	2-2	2-2	1-0	1-1	4-0	2-1	4-1	0-1	1-1	1-3	1-0	■	1-2	0-1	2-5	2-1
Thurrock	1-2	0-3	0-1	1-3	0-1	5-1	0-2	1-0	0-0	3-0	1-1	1-2	4-0	0-3	2-0	1-2	1-1	0-4	■	0-0	0-3	1-2
Wealdstone	1-0	2-3	2-0	3-0	2-1	2-0	1-1	4-0	3-2	2-0	3-0	2-1	5-2	2-0	6-1	0-0	2-1	1-0	2-2	■	1-1	2-3
Whitehawk	3-0	2-2	5-4	2-0	1-0	2-0	1-0	6-0	0-0	0-0	2-2	0-0	2-0	5-1	3-1	1-3	1-1	1-1	5-1	1-1	■	3-1
Wingate & Finchley	1-3	1-3	0-1	1-0	0-0	4-4	0-1	1-2	0-3	2-1	2-2	0-1	3-0	2-2	2-4	3-2	1-0	1-3	0-1	1-1	2-3	■

Ryman League Premier Division

Season 2012/2013

	P	W	D	L	F	A	Pts
Whitehawk	42	25	13	4	88	42	88
Lowestoft Town	42	23	11	8	71	38	80
Wealdstone	42	22	13	7	70	38	79
Concord Rangers	42	22	10	10	80	54	76
East Thurrock United	42	18	16	8	65	45	70
Metropolitan Police	42	20	10	12	65	56	70
Bury Town	42	19	9	14	66	64	66
Canvey Island	42	18	10	14	60	55	64
Margate	42	17	11	14	61	49	62
Hendon	42	16	12	14	48	50	60
Kingstonian	42	18	5	19	63	62	59
Leiston	42	13	17	12	57	57	56
Hampton & Richmond	42	13	14	15	58	56	53
Bognor Regis Town	42	15	8	19	48	58	53
Harrow Borough	42	12	9	21	53	71	45
Enfield Town	42	13	5	24	60	83	44
Cray Wanderers	42	10	13	19	60	85	43
Wingate & Finchley	42	12	6	24	56	82	42
Lewes	42	9	13	20	59	75	40
Carshalton Athletic	42	12	4	26	55	76	40
Hastings United	42	8	15	19	39	62	39
Thurrock	42	11	8	23	40	62	38

Thurrock had three points deducted after the end of the season for fielding an ineligible player. A subsequent appeal was rejected.

Promotion Play-offs

Lowestoft Town 1   East Thurrock United 0
Wealdstone 1   Concord Rangers .... 2 (aet)

Lowestoft Town 1   Concord Rangers 2

Promoted: Billericay Town and AFC Hornchurch

Relegated: Hastings United and Thurrock

F.A. Trophy 2012/2013

Qualifying 1	AFC Fylde	1	Marine	0
Qualifying 1	AFC Totton	2	Bideford	0
Qualifying 1	Banbury United	1	Wimborne Town	1
Qualifying 1	Barton Rovers	0	Coalville Town	5
Qualifying 1	Belper Town	2	Leamington	2
Qualifying 1	Bishop's Cleeve	1	Chesham United	2
Qualifying 1	Bognor Regis Town	4	Ilford	1
Qualifying 1	Bridgwater Town	2	Hemel Hempstead Town	2
Qualifying 1	Burnham	4	Waltham Abbey	3
Qualifying 1	Burscough	3	Wakefield	2
Qualifying 1	Bury Town	0	Whitehawk	0
Qualifying 1	Cammell Laird	1	Kendal Town	1
Qualifying 1	Canvey Island	0	Wroxham	0
Qualifying 1	Carshalton Athletic	3	Heybridge Swifts	0
Qualifying 1	Chasetown	3	St. Neots Town	2
Qualifying 1	Chatham Town	2	Merstham	4
Qualifying 1	Chippenham Town	4	Swindon Supermarine	0
Qualifying 1	Chorley	1	Whitby Town	3
Qualifying 1	Crawley Down	1	Three Bridges	2
Qualifying 1	Curzon Ashton	2	Worksop Town	3
Qualifying 1	Didcot Town	3	Cinderford Town	1
Qualifying 1	East Thurrock United	4	Hastings United	0
Qualifying 1	Eastwood Town	1	Matlock Town	2
Qualifying 1	Enfield Town	4	Cambridge City	1
Qualifying 1	FC United of Manchester	3	Mossley	3
Qualifying 1	Faversham Town	0	Leatherhead	2
Qualifying 1	Frickley Athletic	1	North Ferriby United	4
Qualifying 1	Frome Town	0	Taunton Town	1
Qualifying 1	Grantham Town	0	Bedford Town	2
Qualifying 1	Grays Athletic	1	Ashford Town (Middlesex)	1
Qualifying 1	Halesowen Town	3	Gresley	0
Qualifying 1	Hampton & Richmond Borough	1	Hythe Town	1
Qualifying 1	Harrogate Railway Athletic	2	Trafford	4
Qualifying 1	Hednesford Town	3	Bedworth United	1
Qualifying 1	Hitchin Town	3	Sittingbourne	1
Qualifying 1	Hucknall Town	2	Newcastle Town	1
Qualifying 1	Kettering Town	0	Concord Rangers	3
Qualifying 1	King's Lynn Town	1	Barwell	0
Qualifying 1	Kingstonian	2	Eastbourne Town	1
Qualifying 1	Leek Town	2	Radcliffe Borough	1
Qualifying 1	Leiston	2	Hendon	1
Qualifying 1	Lewes	1	Lowestoft Town	0
Qualifying 1	Lincoln United	0	Buxton	4
Qualifying 1	Margate	1	Maidstone United	2
Qualifying 1	Merthyr Town	1	Chalfont St. Peter	0
Qualifying 1	Nantwich Town	2	Redditch United	1
Qualifying 1	New Mills	3	Stocksbridge Park Steels	2
Qualifying 1	North Leigh	2	Sholing	2
Qualifying 1	Ossett Town	1	Ashton United	0
Qualifying 1	Poole Town	1	Bashley	1
Qualifying 1	Prescot Cables	0	Skelmersdale United	3
Qualifying 1	Ramsbottom United	4	Northwich Victoria	2
Qualifying 1	Ramsgate	4	Waltham Forest	0
Qualifying 1	Redbridge	0	Metropolitan Police	5

Qualifying 1	Romford	1	Thurrock	3	
Qualifying 1	Romulus	2	Rainworth MW	0	
Qualifying 1	Rugby Town	1	Stafford Rangers	1	
Qualifying 1	Rushall Olympic	3	Woodford United	0	
Qualifying 1	Shortwood United	4	Guildford City	0	
Qualifying 1	Slough Town	0	Gosport Borough	4	
Qualifying 1	Soham Town Rangers	2	Tooting & Mitcham United	0	
Qualifying 1	St. Albans City	1	Arlesey Town	2	
Qualifying 1	Stamford	3	Kidsgrove Athletic	1	
Qualifying 1	Stourbridge	0	Ilkeston FC	1	
Qualifying 1	Thamesmead Town	0	Cray Wanderers	1	
Qualifying 1	Uxbridge	2	Royston Town	2	
Qualifying 1	Walton & Hersham	1	Brentwood Town	2	
Qualifying 1	Wealdstone	3	Chertsey Town	1	
Qualifying 1	Weymouth	3	Tiverton Town	0	
Qualifying 1	Whitstable Town	2	Harrow Borough	0	
Qualifying 1	Wingate & Finchley	2	Potters Bar Town	1	
Qualifying 1	Witton Albion	4	Blyth Spartans	1	
Replay	Ashford Town (Middlesex)	1	Grays Athletic	2	
Replay	Bashley	0	Poole Town	4	
Replay	Hemel Hempstead Town	1	Bridgwater Town	3	
Replay	Hythe Town	0	Hampton & Richmond Borough	4	
Replay	Kendal Town	0	Cammell Laird	2	
Replay	Leamington	2	Belper Town	2	(aet)
	Belper Town won 4-3 on penalties				
Replay	Mossley	1	FC United of Manchester	3	
Replay	Royston Town	1	Uxbridge	3	
Replay	Sholing	4	North Leigh	3	
Replay	Stafford Rangers	1	Rugby Town	0	(aet)
Replay	Whitehawk	1	Bury Town	0	
Replay	Wimborne Town	3	Banbury United	3	(aet)
	Wimborne Town won 6-5 on penalties				
Replay	Wroxham	1	Canvey Island	2	(aet)
Qualifying 2	AFC Fylde	0	Nantwich Town	0	
Qualifying 2	AFC Totton	3	Gosport Borough	2	
Qualifying 2	Bedford Town	2	Maidstone United	3	
Qualifying 2	Belper Town	0	Cammell Laird	2	
Qualifying 2	Bognor Regis Town	3	Bridgwater Town	0	
Qualifying 2	Brentwood Town	3	Lewes	3	
Qualifying 2	Burscough	0	Ossett Town	1	
Qualifying 2	Buxton	2	North Ferriby United	1	
Qualifying 2	Chasetown	1	Rushall Olympic	3	
Qualifying 2	Chesham United	5	Taunton Town	1	
Qualifying 2	Chippenham Town	1	Sholing	2	
Qualifying 2	Concord Rangers	0	Enfield Town	2	
Qualifying 2	Cray Wanderers	0	Arlesey Town	0	
Qualifying 2	East Thurrock United	1	Thurrock	1	
Qualifying 2	Halesowen Town	0	Worksop Town	1	
Qualifying 2	Hampton & Richmond Borough	1	Three Bridges	0	
Qualifying 2	King's Lynn Town	6	Carshalton Athletic	1	
Qualifying 2	Kingstonian	2	Burnham	1	
Qualifying 2	Leiston	1	Metropolitan Police	1	
Qualifying 2	Matlock Town	0	Leek Town	0	
Qualifying 2	Merstham	2	Wealdstone	6	
Qualifying 2	New Mills	5	Coalville Town	2	
Qualifying 2	Poole Town	1	Didcot Town	1	
Qualifying 2	Romulus	1	Hucknall Town	0	

Qualifying 2	Soham Town Rangers	1	Ramsgate	2	
Qualifying 2	Stafford Rangers	3	Ramsbottom United	0	
Qualifying 2	Stamford	2	FC United of Manchester	1	
Qualifying 2	Trafford	0	Hednesford Town	2	
Qualifying 2	Uxbridge	3	Canvey Island	3	
Qualifying 2	Weymouth	1	Shortwood United	2	
Qualifying 2	Whitby Town	4	Ilkeston FC	2	
Qualifying 2	Whitehawk	1	Grays Athletic	1	
Qualifying 2	Whitstable Town	0	Leatherhead	1	
Qualifying 2	Wimborne Town	1	Merthyr Town	5	
Qualifying 2	Wingate & Finchley	2	Hitchin Town	2	
Qualifying 2	Witton Albion	2	Skelmersdale United	3	
Replay	Arlesey Town	2	Cray Wanderers	3	(aet)
Replay	Canvey Island	4	Uxbridge	2	
Replay	Didcot Town	2	Poole Town	0	
Replay	Grays Athletic	0	Whitehawk	1	
Replay	Hitchin Town	3	Wingate & Finchley	0	
Replay	Leek Town	1	Matlock Town	3	
Replay	Lewes	0	Brentwood Town	3	
Replay	Metropolitan Police	3	Leiston	4	
Replay	Nantwich Town	2	AFC Fylde	2	(aet)
	AFC Fylde won 3-1 on penalties				
Replay	Thurrock	4	East Thurrock United	3	(aet)
Qualifying 3	AFC Hornchurch	2	Bishop's Stortford	3	
Qualifying 3	AFC Totton	3	Basingstoke Town	0	
Qualifying 3	Billericay Town	3	Enfield Town	2	
Qualifying 3	Bognor Regis Town	1	Havant & Waterlooville	4	
Qualifying 3	Boston United	3	Colwyn Bay	1	
Qualifying 3	Bromley	1	Staines Town	1	
Qualifying 3	Cammell Laird	0	FC Halifax Town	1	
Qualifying 3	Canvey Island	1	Chesham United	1	
Qualifying 3	Chelmsford City	1	Dover Athletic	1	
Qualifying 3	Chester FC	2	Worksop Town	2	
Qualifying 3	Cray Wanderers	0	Welling United	1	
Qualifying 3	Didcot Town	1	Dorchester Town	2	
Qualifying 3	Droylsden	1	Rushall Olympic	2	
Qualifying 3	Eastleigh	1	Hayes & Yeading United	4	
Qualifying 3	Farnborough	3	Truro City	2	
Qualifying 3	Gainsborough Trinity	1	Hinckley United	1	
Qualifying 3	Gloucester City	0	Maidenhead United	1	
Qualifying 3	Guiseley	7	Whitby Town	0	
Qualifying 3	Histon	1	Boreham Wood	2	
Qualifying 3	King's Lynn Town	3	Eastbourne Borough	0	
Qualifying 3	Kingstonian	2	Brentwood Town	2	
Qualifying 3	Leatherhead	4	Bath City	4	
Qualifying 3	Leiston	1	Hampton & Richmond Borough	1	
Qualifying 3	Maidstone United	3	Whitehawk	2	
Qualifying 3	Matlock Town	2	Stalybridge Celtic	1	
Qualifying 3	Ossett Town	2	Workington	1	
Qualifying 3	Romulus	1	Hednesford Town	2	
Qualifying 3	Salisbury City	3	Weston-Super-Mare	0	
Qualifying 3	Sholing	0	Oxford City	1	
Qualifying 3	Shortwood United	1	Merthyr Town	1	
Qualifying 3	Skelmersdale United	3	New Mills	1	
Qualifying 3	Solihull Moors	2	AFC Fylde	1	
Qualifying 3	Stafford Rangers	3	Bradford Park Avenue	1	

Qualifying 3	Stamford	0	Buxton	2	
Qualifying 3	Sutton United	2	Ramsgate	0	
Qualifying 3	Thurrock	0	Brackley Town	2	
Qualifying 3	Tonbridge Angels	2	Hitchin Town	1	
Qualifying 3	Vauxhall Motors	1	Harrogate Town	3	
Qualifying 3	Wealdstone	1	Corby Town	1	
Qualifying 3	Worcester City	0	Altrincham	3	
Replay	Bath City	2	Leatherhead	0	
Replay	Brentwood Town	1	Kingstonian	4	
Replay	Chesham United	2	Canvey Island	1	
Replay	Corby Town	3	Wealdstone	2	
Replay	Dover Athletic	2	Chelmsford City	4	(aet)
Replay	Hampton & Richmond Borough	3	Leiston	2	
Replay	Hinckley United	1	Gainsborough Trinity	4	
Replay	Merthyr Town	2	Shortwood United	1	
Replay	Staines Town	0	Bromley	2	
Replay	Worksop Town	2	Chester FC	0	
Round 1	AFC Telford United	1	Nuneaton Town	0	
Round 1	Alfreton Town	1	Kidderminster Harriers	3	
Round 1	Billericay Town	0	Cambridge United	3	
Round 1	Boston United	1	Skelmersdale United	1	
Round 1	Braintree Town	1	Havant & Waterlooville	2	
Round 1	Bromley	1	Boreham Wood	1	
Round 1	Chesham United	2	Bath City	1	
Round 1	Corby Town	3	Hayes & Yeading United	2	
Round 1	Dorchester Town	2	Luton Town	2	
Round 1	Ebbsfleet United	0	Hereford United	1	
Round 1	FC Halifax Town	5	Altrincham	2	
Round 1	Forest Green Rovers	2	AFC Totton	1	
Round 1	Gainsborough Trinity	2	Harrogate Town	0	
Round 1	Gateshead	2	Macclesfield Town	0	
Round 1	Grimsby Town	0	Buxton	0	
Round 1	Guiseley	3	Brackley Town	1	
Round 1	Hampton & Richmond Borough	1	Chelmsford City	1	
Round 1	Hednesford Town	1	Solihull Moors	2	
Round 1	Hyde	1	Barrow	1	
Round 1	Kingstonian	0	Dartford	4	
Round 1	Maidenhead United	0	Sutton United	1	
Round 1	Maidstone United	2	Salisbury City	0	
Round 1	Mansfield Town	1	Matlock Town	1	
Round 1	Merthyr Town	1	Tonbridge Angels	2	
Round 1	Oxford City	1	Bishop's Stortford	0	
Round 1	Stafford Rangers	0	Southport	4	
Round 1	Stockport County	6	Ossett Town	0	
Round 1	Tamworth	3	Lincoln City	1	
Round 1	Welling United	2	Newport County	0	
Round 1	Woking	7	Farnborough	0	
Round 1	Worksop Town	0	King's Lynn Town	1	
Round 1	Wrexham	5	Rushall Olympic	0	
Replay	Barrow	1	Hyde	0	
Replay	Boreham Wood	0	Bromley	2	
Replay	Buxton	0	Grimsby Town	1	
Replay	Chelmsford City	3	Hampton & Richmond Borough	2	
Replay	Luton Town	3	Dorchester Town	1	
Replay	Matlock Town	2	Mansfield Town	1	
Replay	Skelmersdale United	2	Boston United	1	

Round 2	Bromley	1	Kidderminster Harriers	0
Round 2	Cambridge United	0	Gateshead	1
Round 2	Chesham United	1	Barrow	5
Round 2	Dartford	3	Tonbridge Angels	0
Round 2	FC Halifax Town	2	Maidstone United	1
Round 2	Forest Green Rovers	1	Gainsborough Trinity	2
Round 2	Grimsby Town	4	Havant & Waterlooville	0
Round 2	Hereford United	0	Chelmsford City	3
Round 2	King's Lynn Town	3	AFC Telford United	1
Round 2	Matlock Town	1	Luton Town	2
Round 2	Skelmersdale United	2	Guiseley	0
Round 2	Stockport County	1	Southport	1
Round 2	Sutton United	1	Oxford City	0
Round 2	Tamworth	1	Corby Town	1
Round 2	Woking	0	Welling United	1
Round 2	Wrexham	3	Solihull Moors	2
Replay	Corby Town	2	Tamworth	4
Replay	Southport	3	Stockport County	1
Round 3	Dartford	4	Bromley	2
Round 3	FC Halifax Town	3	Chelmsford City	0
Round 3	Gainsborough Trinity	2	Tamworth	1
Round 3	Gateshead	2	Barrow	3
Round 3	King's Lynn Town	0	Southport	2
Round 3	Luton Town	2	Skelmersdale United	0
Round 3	Sutton United	0	Wrexham	5
Round 3	Welling United	1	Grimsby Town	2
Round 4	Dartford	3	FC Halifax Town	2
Round 4	FC Halifax Town	1	Dartford	1
Round 4	Gainsborough Trinity	2	Barrow	0
Round 4	Grimsby Town	3	Luton Town	0
Round 4	Southport	1	Wrexham	3
Semi-finals				
1st leg	Grimsby Town	3	Dartford	0
2nd leg	Dartford	0	Grimsby Town	0
	Grimsby Town won 3-0 on aggregate			
1st leg	Wrexham	3	Gainsborough Trinity	1
2nd leg	Gainsborough Trinity	2	Wrexham	1
	Wrexham won 4-3 on aggregate			
FINAL	Wrexham	1	Grimsby Town	1	(aet)
	Wrexham won 4-1 on penalties			

F.A. Vase 2012/2013

Round 1	AFC Dunstable	1	Hatfield Town	3	
Round 1	AFC Emley	1	Congleton Town	0	
Round 1	AFC Liverpool	1	Armthorpe Welfare	3	
Round 1	AFC St. Austell	4	Bovey Tracey	3	
Round 1	AFC Wulfrunians	3	Tipton Town	0	
Round 1	Amersham Town	4	Flackwell Heath	3	(aet)
Round 1	Aylesbury United	0	Kidlington	2	
Round 1	Barking	0	Dunstable Town	3	
Round 1	Barnoldswick Town	4	Maine Road	2	
Round 1	Bartley Green	0	Shawbury United	5	
Round 1	Blackfield & Langley	5	Westbury United	1	
Round 1	Bodmin Town	3	Brislington	2	
Round 1	Bootle	3	Stockport Sports	2	
Round 1	Bottesford Town	2	Rochdale Town	1	
Round 1	Bridgnorth Town	3	Shifnal Town	1	(aet)
Round 1	Bridlington Town	1	Spennymoor Town	5	
Round 1	Burnham Ramblers	3	Gorleston	1	
Round 1	Cadbury Heath	3	Hayling United	2	
Round 1	Causeway United	2	Stourport Swifts	0	
Round 1	Cheadle Town	1	Wigan Robin Park	3	
Round 1	Cheltenham Saracens	1	Ardley United	2	
Round 1	Christchurch	1	Horndean	3	(aet)
Round 1	Clapton	0	Cockfosters	3	
Round 1	Colney Heath	3	Sporting Bengal United	2	
Round 1	Coventry Sphinx	5	Bilston Town	4	(aet)
Round 1	Deal Town	2	Hassocks	0	
Round 1	Deeping Rangers	2	Quorn	1	
Round 1	Dereham Town	4	Stewarts & Lloyds	1	
Round 1	Downton	2	Petersfield Town	1	
Round 1	Dunkirk	1	Boston Town	2	
Round 1	Egham Town	2	Lordswood	3	
Round 1	Ely City	2	Eynesbury Rovers	0	
Round 1	Erith Town	3	AFC Croydon Athletic	2	
Round 1	Exmouth Town	1	Sherborne Town	2	
Round 1	Fawley	2	Bemerton Heath Harlequins	2	
Round 1	Frimley Green	2	Canterbury City	1	(aet)
Round 1	GE Hamble	3	Bristol Academy	1	
Round 1	Godmanchester Rovers	1	Cambridge University Press	3	(aet)
Round 1	Graham Street Primitives	2	Holbrook Sports	3	
Round 1	Greenwood Meadows	3	Borrowash Victoria	3	(aet)
Round 1	Hadleigh United	1	Walsham Le Willows	1	(aet)
Round 1	Hadley	4	Berkhamsted	4	(aet)
Round 1	Hall Road Rangers	2	Brighouse Town	5	
Round 1	Hanworth Villa	2	Wembley	0	
Round 1	Haverhill Rovers	0	Southend Manor	2	
Round 1	Haverhill Sports Association	3	Ipswich Wanderers	2	
Round 1	Heather St. Johns	0	Long Eaton United	1	
Round 1	Hoddesdon Town	3	Hertford Town	5	
Round 1	Holyport	1	Newbury	4	
Round 1	Hullbridge Sports	0	Diss Town	2	
Round 1	Jarrow Roofing Boldon CA	1	Norton & Stockton Ancients	0	
Round 1	Kirby Muxloe	1	Basford United	4	
Round 1	Lancing	0	Peacehaven & Telscombe	5	
Round 1	Lingfield	1	Colliers Wood United	2	
Round 1	Littlehampton Town	2	Beckenham Town	1	

Round 1	London Lions	2	Codicote	1	(aet)
Round 1	Long Buckby	2	Northampton Spencer	2	(aet)
Round 1	Long Melford	0	Brantham Athletic	8	
Round 1	Longwell Green Sports	2	Calne Town	0	
Round 1	Lye Town	1	Gornal Athletic	3	
Round 1	Moneyfields	6	Hallen	0	
Round 1	Morpeth Town	1	Guisborough Town	0	(aet)
Round 1	New Milton Town	2	Alton Town	1	
Round 1	Newton Aycliffe	1	Esh Winning	2	
Round 1	Northallerton Town	1	Consett	1	(aet)
Round 1	Nostell MW	1	Formby	2	
Round 1	Oxford City Nomads	2	Windsor	1	
Round 1	Oxhey Jets	1	Hanwell Town	1	(aet)
Round 1	Pagham	2	Horsham YMCA	2	(aet)
Round 1	Pegasus Juniors	1	Southam United	2	
Round 1	Penrith	1	Bedlington Terriers	2	
Round 1	Pickering Town	4	Durham City	1	
Round 1	Rocester	4	Bewdley Town	0	
Round 1	Runcorn Linnets	1	Winsford United	3	
Round 1	Rye United	3	Horley Town	2	
Round 1	Saltash United	0	Buckland Athletic	1	
Round 1	Sandhurst Town	1	Wantage Town	8	
Round 1	Sevenoaks Town	2	Ash United	4	
Round 1	Shepshed Dynamo	2	Blidworth Welfare	0	
Round 1	Shirebrook Town	1	Heanor Town	1	(aet)
Round 1	South Shields	2	Shildon	3	
Round 1	Spalding United	3	Retford United	2	
Round 1	St. Blazey	2	Barnstaple Town	1	
Round 1	St. Francis Rangers	0	Croydon	2	
Round 1	St. Helens Town	2	Parkgate	4	(aet)
Round 1	Street	0	Odd Down	1	
Round 1	Sunderland RCA	1	Bishop Auckland	0	
Round 1	Sutton Town	3	Sleaford Town	1	
Round 1	Swaffham Town	0	Desborough Town	6	
Round 1	Swanage Town & Herston	0	Newport (IOW)	2	
Round 1	Takeley	3	Great Wakering Rovers	2	(aet)
Round 1	Thackley	3	Scarborough Athletic	2	
Round 1	Thame United	3	Fairford Town	2	
Round 1	VCD Athletic	0	Erith & Belvedere	0	(aet)
Round 1	Walsall Wood	2	Eccleshall	0	
Round 1	Westfields	1	Black Country Rangers	4	
Round 1	Whitton United	0	Brightlingsea Regent	1	
Round 1	Whyteleafe	2	Guernsey	3	
Round 1	Witney Town	0	Ascot United	2	
Round 1	Wokingham & Emmbrook	0	Marlow	1	(aet)
Round 1	Yaxley	1	AFC Rushden & Diamonds	2	
Replay	Berkhamsted	2	Hadley	0	
Replay	Borrowash Victoria	5	Greenwood Meadows	2	(aet)
Replay	Consett	3	Northallerton Town	2	
Replay	Erith & Belvedere	3	VCD Athletic	2	
Replay	Hanwell Town	0	Oxhey Jets	1	
Replay	Heanor Town	2	Shirebrook Town	4	
Replay	Horsham YMCA	1	Pagham	0	
Replay	Northampton Spencer	1	Long Buckby	0	
Replay	Walsham Le Willows	0	Hadleigh United	2	(aet)
Round 2	AFC Emley	3	Bottesford Town	2	

Round 2	AFC Rushden & Diamonds	5	Basford United	3	
Round 2	AFC St. Austell	2	Bemerton Heath Harlequins	3	
Round 2	AFC Wulfrunians	5	Shawbury United	3	(aet)
Round 2	Amersham Town	1	Rye United	0	

Amersham Town were subsequently disqualified from the competition. Rye United progressed.

Round 2	Ampthill Town	1	Diss Town	0	
Round 2	Ascot United	3	Reading Town	0	
Round 2	Ash United	0	South Park	2	
Round 2	Ashington	2	Sunderland RCA	1	
Round 2	Barnoldswick Town	5	Armthorpe Welfare	2	
Round 2	Bedlington Terriers	1	Wigan Robin Park	2	
Round 2	Berkhamsted	1	Southend Manor	2	
Round 2	Black Country Rangers	2	Holbrook Sports	3	
Round 2	Blackfield & Langley	1	Bournemouth (Ams)	0	
Round 2	Bodmin Town	5	Odd Down	1	
Round 2	Borrowash Victoria	1	Northampton Spencer	0	
Round 2	Brantham Athletic	3	Cambridge University Press	2	
Round 2	Bridgnorth Town	2	Boston Town	3	
Round 2	Buckland Athletic	2	Downton	5	
Round 2	Burnham Ramblers	1	Bethnal Green United	2	
Round 2	Causeway United	2	Desborough Town	1	
Round 2	Colliers Wood United	w/o	Old Woodstock Town		

Old Woodstock Town were expelled from the competition as their ground did not comply with regulations.

Round 2	Colney Heath	1	Hadleigh United	2	
Round 2	Consett	2	Shildon	3	
Round 2	Coventry Sphinx	1	Gornal Athletic	8	
Round 2	Croydon	9	Newbury	2	
Round 2	Deal Town	2	Binfield	5	
Round 2	Deeping Rangers	0	Norton United	1	
Round 2	Dunston UTS	5	West Auckland Town	0	
Round 2	Erith & Belvedere	5	Frimley Green	1	
Round 2	Erith Town	3	Guernsey	4	(aet)
Round 2	Hatfield Town	3	Ely City	7	
Round 2	Haverhill Sports Association	2	Dereham Town	1	
Round 2	Horndean	4	Willand Rovers	3	(aet)
Round 2	Horsham YMCA	0	Ardley United	1	
Round 2	Larkhall Athletic	0	Longwell Green Sports	0	(aet)
Round 2	Littlehampton Town	1	Hanworth Villa	1	(aet)
Round 2	London Lions	2	Brightlingsea Regent	3	
Round 2	Marlow	2	Kidlington	4	
Round 2	Moneyfields	0	GE Hamble	1	
Round 2	New Milton Town	1	Bitton	2	
Round 2	Newport (IOW)	1	Cadbury Heath	0	
Round 2	Newport Pagnell Town	1	Enfield 1893	2	
Round 2	Oadby Town	2	Spalding United	3	
Round 2	Oxford City Nomads	0	Peacehaven & Telscombe	3	
Round 2	Oxhey Jets	4	Cockfosters	0	
Round 2	Parkgate	4	Esh Winning	2	
Round 2	Peterborough Northern Star	1	Dunstable Town	3	
Round 2	Pickering Town	2	Billingham Synthonia	3	
Round 2	Runcorn Town	2	Formby	1	
Round 2	Shepshed Dynamo	1	Rocester	3	
Round 2	Sherborne Town	1	St. Blazey	4	
Round 2	Shirebrook Town	3	Walsall Wood	3	(aet)
Round 2	Southam United	0	Long Eaton United	1	
Round 2	Spennymoor Town	5	Newcastle Benfield	1	
Round 2	St. Ives Town	2	Wisbech Town	2	(aet)

Round 2	Staveley MW	1	Brighouse Town	3	(aet)
Round 2	Sutton Town	2	Tividale	1	
Round 2	Takeley	0	Hertford Town	1	
Round 2	Thackley	3	Bootle	1	
Round 2	Thame United	2	Lordswood	3	
Round 2	Tunbridge Wells	2	Wantage Town	0	
Round 2	Whitley Bay	2	Jarrow Roofing Boldon CA	1	
Round 2	Winsford United	1	Morpeth Town	0	
Replay	Hanworth Villa	2	Littlehampton Town	1	
Replay	Longwell Green Sports	1	Larkhall Athletic	2	
Replay	Walsall Wood	3	Shirebrook Town	0	
Replay	Wisbech Town	2	St. Ives Town	1	
Round 3	AFC Wulfrunians	2	Borrowash Victoria	3	(aet)
Round 3	Ampthill Town	1	Hertford Town	0	
Round 3	Ardley United	1	Newport (IOW)	4	
Round 3	Ashington	2	AFC Rushden & Diamonds	1	
Round 3	Barnoldswick Town	1	AFC Emley	3	
Round 3	Bethnal Green United	1	Ely City	3	
Round 3	Binfield	1	Tunbridge Wells	2	
Round 3	Bodmin Town	2	Downton	0	
Round 3	Brighouse Town	4	Holbrook Sports	1	
Round 3	Brightlingsea Regent	2	Brantham Athletic	3	
Round 3	Colliers Wood United	2	Ascot United	3	
Round 3	Croydon	0	Hanworth Villa	2	
Round 3	Enfield 1893	1	Dunstable Town	0	
Round 3	GE Hamble	0	Blackfield & Langley	2	
Round 3	Gornal Athletic	1	Boston Town	0	
Round 3	Guernsey	4	Erith & Belvedere	0	
Round 3	Hadleigh United	2	Oxhey Jets	0	
Round 3	Haverhill Sports Association	3	Peacehaven & Telscombe	4	
Round 3	Horndean	0	Bemerton Heath Harlequins	5	
Round 3	Larkhall Athletic	3	Kidlington	2	
Round 3	Lordswood	3	Southend Manor	0	
Round 3	Norton United	0	Dunston UTS	2	
Round 3	Rocester	2	Long Eaton United	1	
Round 3	Rye United	1	South Park	0	
Round 3	Shildon	3	Parkgate	1	
Round 3	Spennymoor Town	2	Billingham Synthonia	0	
Round 3	St. Blazey	0	Bitton	3	
Round 3	Sutton Town	1	Spalding United	5	
Round 3	Thackley	2	Wisbech Town	4	
Round 3	Walsall Wood	4	Wigan Robin Park	1	
Round 3	Whitley Bay	6	Causeway United	0	
Round 3	Winsford United	1	Runcorn Town	3	
Round 4	AFC Emley	0	Hadleigh United	1	
Round 4	Ampthill Town	3	Enfield 1893	0	
Round 4	Bemerton Heath Harlequins	3	Blackfield & Langley	2	
Round 4	Bitton	0	Shildon	2	
Round 4	Bodmin Town	3	Ashington	2	
Round 4	Borrowash Victoria	0	Ascot United	3	
Round 4	Brantham Athletic	1	Whitley Bay	0	(aet)
Round 4	Ely City	1	Spalding United	2	
Round 4	Gornal Athletic	4	Wisbech Town	2	(aet)
Round 4	Hanworth Villa	2	Walsall Wood	3	
Round 4	Larkhall Athletic	2	Peacehaven & Telscombe	1	
Round 4	Newport (IOW)	2	Brighouse Town	1	

Round 4	Rocester	1	Runcorn Town	2	
Round 4	Rye United	5	Guernsey	6	(aet)
Round 4	Spennymoor Town	3	Lordswood	1	
Round 4	Tunbridge Wells	1	Dunston UTS	0	
Round 5	Ampthill Town	1	Hadleigh United	2	
Round 5	Ascot United	2	Newport (IOW)	2	(aet)
Round 5	Bodmin Town	0	Gornal Athletic	1	
Round 5	Brantham Athletic	1	Shildon	4	
Round 5	Larkhall Athletic	3	Tunbridge Wells	4	(aet)
Round 5	Runcorn Town	1	Walsall Wood	2	(aet)
Round 5	Spalding United	1	Guernsey	3	
Round 5	Spennymoor Town	4	Bemerton Heath Harlequins	2	
Replay	Ascot United	2	Newport (IOW)	1	
Round 6	Shildon	1	Ascot United	1	(aet)
Round 6	Spennymoor Town	3	Gornal Athletic	1	
Round 6	Tunbridge Wells	2	Hadleigh United	0	
Round 6	Walsall Wood	0	Guernsey	0	(aet)
Replay	Ascot United	1	Shildon	4	
Replay	Guernsey	3	Walsall Wood	1	
Semi-finals					
1st leg	Guernsey	1	Spennymoor Town	3	
2nd leg	Spennymoor Town	1	Guernsey	0	
	Spennymoor Town won 4-1 on aggregate				
1st leg	Tunbridge Wells	2	Shildon	0	
2nd leg	Shildon	3	Tunbridge Wells	2	
	Tunbridge Wells won 4-2 on aggregate				
FINAL	Spennymoor Town	9	Tunbridge Wells	9	

Football Conference National Fixtures 2013/2014 Season	Aldershot Town	Alfreton Town	Barnet	Braintree Town	Cambridge United	Chester	Dartford	FC Halifax Town	Forest Green Rovers	Gateshead	Grimsby Town	Hereford United	Hyde United	Kidderminster Harriers	Lincoln City	Luton Town	Macclesfield Town	Nuneaton Town	Salisbury City	Southport	Tamworth	Welling United	Woking	Wrexham
Aldershot Town		19/10	17/09	09/11	17/08	08/02	13/08	25/01	01/01	25/03	05/10	26/04	29/03	18/01	01/03	08/10	07/09	15/03	19/04	23/11	21/12	28/12	26/08	21/09
Alfreton Town	15/02		21/09	16/11	17/09	08/10	21/12	02/11	05/10	22/02	19/04	26/08	01/02	13/08	08/03	07/12	26/04	29/03	17/08	28/12	18/01	05/04	07/09	01/01
Barnet	14/12	04/01		21/04	16/11	10/08	07/12	12/04	05/04	08/03	11/01	22/03	31/08	02/11	14/09	26/12	24/09	24/08	28/09	25/01	15/02	12/11	01/03	12/10
Braintree Town	22/03	28/09	26/08		01/01	19/10	19/04	23/11	07/09	25/01	26/04	08/03	01/03	17/08	18/01	12/11	21/12	08/02	05/04	21/09	28/12	08/10	13/08	15/02
Cambridge United	12/11	11/01	29/03	26/12		21/04	15/03	10/08	21/09	14/09	04/01	05/10	12/04	01/03	24/08	14/12	09/11	24/09	19/10	05/04	31/08	15/02	23/11	01/02
Chester	02/11	15/03	18/01	07/12	12/10		07/09	15/02	26/08	28/12	21/09	13/08	05/04	05/10	21/12	16/11	17/09	01/03	26/04	01/01	25/03	01/02	17/08	19/04
Dartford	11/01	10/08	09/11	24/08	25/01	08/03		14/12	12/04	23/11	15/02	22/02	19/10	21/09	31/08	01/02	29/03	14/09	08/10	28/09	21/04	26/12	28/12	19/11
FC Halifax Town	16/11	22/03	07/09	18/02	18/01	28/09	17/08		21/12	01/01	17/09	21/09	12/11	26/04	28/12	29/03	19/04	08/10	07/12	26/08	01/03	19/10	08/02	13/08
Forest Green Rovers	26/12	31/08	08/02	14/12	08/03	25/01	02/11	14/09		28/09	07/12	11/01	10/08	08/04	16/11	24/08	12/10	12/11	04/01	22/02	24/09	22/03	19/04	26/04
Gateshead	07/12	12/10	17/08	29/03	26/04	24/09	05/10	26/12	01/03		13/08	07/09	04/01	01/02	22/03	02/11	26/08	11/01	16/11	19/04	05/04	14/12	15/02	17/09
Grimsby Town	10/08	24/08	23/11	14/09	08/10	12/04	24/09	22/02	19/10	18/01		01/02	21/04	20/12	01/01	25/03	28/12	31/08	01/03	08/02	28/09	09/11	08/04	15/03
Hereford United	14/09	21/04	19/10	10/08	21/12	12/11	12/10	09/11	28/12	12/04	29/03		15/03	01/01	24/09	28/09	08/02	07/12	25/01	18/01	24/08	31/08	05/04	01/03
Hyde United	22/02	23/11	21/12	05/10	07/09	09/11	22/03	08/03	18/01	08/10	26/08	17/08		19/04	08/02	26/04	01/01	02/11	08/04	13/08	25/01	21/09	17/09	28/12
Kidderminster Harr.	28/09	14/12	15/03	22/02	08/02	24/08	04/01	24/09	08/10	10/08	05/04	26/12	14/09		19/10	31/08	25/01	21/04	11/01	22/03	23/11	12/04	09/11	16/11
Lincoln City	12/10	19/11	26/04	15/03	19/04	22/02	05/04	01/02	17/08	09/11	26/12	23/11	28/09	15/02		04/01	13/08	14/12	07/09	17/09	08/10	11/01	25/01	26/08
Luton Town	05/04	01/03	01/01	12/04	26/08	22/03	17/09	05/10	21/04	21/12	07/09	15/02	12/10	28/12	21/09		17/08	25/01	13/08	09/11	08/02	23/11	15/03	18/01
Macclesfield Town	12/04	14/09	01/02	31/08	01/04	04/01	16/11	24/08	15/02	21/04	08/03	08/10	26/12	12/11	07/12	11/01		10/08	14/12	19/10	22/03	28/09	21/09	02/11
Nuneaton Town	01/02	09/11	19/04	12/10	28/12	23/11	26/04	05/04	13/08	19/10	22/03	17/09	15/02	26/08	05/10	22/02	18/01		21/09	17/08	01/01	08/03	21/12	07/09
Salisbury City	24/08	08/02	28/12	17/09	22/02	14/09	18/01	31/08	09/11	15/03	12/10	02/11	24/09	29/03	12/04	08/03	23/11	28/01		21/12	10/08	21/04	01/01	05/10
Southport	31/08	24/09	08/04	01/02	02/11	26/12	01/03	21/04	29/03	24/08	14/12	16/11	11/01	12/10	12/11	10/08	15/03	04/01	15/02		12/04	14/09	05/10	07/12
Tamworth	08/03	12/11	13/08	02/11	07/12	11/01	26/08	04/01	15/03	21/09	16/11	19/04	14/12	17/09	29/03	19/10	05/10	26/12	01/02	07/09		22/02	26/04	17/08
Welling United	24/09	25/01	05/10	04/01	13/08	29/03	01/01	15/03	17/09	08/02	17/08	08/04	07/12	07/09	02/11	19/04	01/03	16/11	26/08	26/04	12/10		18/01	21/12
Woking	21/04	12/04	08/10	11/01	22/03	14/12	12/11	12/10	01/02	31/08	02/11	04/01	16/11	07/12	10/08	24/09	22/02	28/09	26/12	08/03	14/09	24/08		29/03
Wrexham	04/01	26/12	22/02	24/09	28/09	31/08	08/02	11/01	23/11	12/11	25/01	14/12	24/08	08/03	21/04	14/09	05/04	12/04	22/03	08/10	09/11	10/08	19/10	

Please note that the above fixtures may be subject to change.

Football Conference North Fixtures 2013/2014 Season	AFC Telford United	Altrincham Town	Barrow	Boston United	Brackley Town	Bradford Park Avenue	Colwyn Bay	Gainsborough Trinity	Gloucester City	Guiseley	Harrogate Town	Hednesford Town	Histon	Leamington	North Ferriby United	Oxford City	Solihull Moors	Stalybridge Celtic	Stockport County	Vauxhall Motors	Worcester City	Workington
AFC Telford United	■	05/04	18/01	28/12	21/12	01/03	21/09	26/04	19/04	01/02	07/09	01/01	15/03	07/12	19/10	22/03	26/08	09/11	15/02	26/10	24/09	17/08
Altrincham Town	11/01	■	20/08	25/01	19/10	08/02	22/02	22/03	24/09	05/10	11/03	02/11	31/08	04/01	12/04	14/09	23/11	26/12	24/08	21/04	14/12	01/03
Barrow	23/11	28/12	■	22/03	17/08	19/04	17/09	07/12	07/09	11/01	26/08	26/04	21/09	01/02	08/02	22/02	21/12	26/10	12/10	29/03	08/03	01/01
Boston United	20/08	26/10	05/10	■	08/02	24/09	09/11	01/02	29/03	14/09	19/10	01/03	26/12	24/08	21/04	15/03	18/01	12/04	14/12	04/01	31/08	30/11
Brackley Town	12/10	08/03	14/12	02/11	■	22/03	05/04	11/01	15/02	04/01	01/03	23/11	20/08	26/12	31/08	21/04	01/02	14/09	12/04	05/10	24/08	25/01
Bradford Park Ave.	14/09	12/10	24/08	23/11	29/03	■	08/03	15/02	02/11	30/11	15/03	18/01	12/04	14/12	19/08	31/08	21/09	21/04	26/12	01/02	04/01	22/02
Colwyn Bay	12/04	29/03	01/03	15/02	30/11	19/10	■	23/11	04/01	24/08	01/02	15/03	14/12	31/08	05/10	11/01	02/11	20/08	21/04	26/12	14/09	01/04
Gainsborough Trin.	31/08	30/11	14/09	12/10	09/11	26/10	25/01	■	15/03	20/08	05/10	05/04	21/04	08/02	26/12	12/04	04/03	24/08	04/01	14/12	22/02	18/01
Gloucester City	24/08	09/11	25/01	21/09	17/09	11/01	26/10	21/12	■	31/08	06/04	07/12	30/11	21/04	22/02	01/01	12/10	22/03	08/03	12/04	20/08	08/02
Guiseley	01/04	21/12	02/11	07/12	07/09	17/09	19/04	28/12	26/04	■	01/01	21/09	19/10	22/02	22/03	23/11	17/08	25/01	18/01	08/03	08/02	26/08
Harrogate Town	04/01	07/12	21/04	22/02	21/09	25/01	22/03	29/03	14/12	26/12	■	08/02	14/09	12/04	24/08	02/11	08/03	11/01	31/08	20/08	09/11	12/10
Hednesford Town	26/12	01/02	31/08	11/01	01/04	09/11	12/10	08/03	05/10	12/04	26/10	■	22/02	20/08	04/01	24/08	15/02	14/12	30/11	14/09	21/04	22/03
Histon	05/10	26/04	05/04	01/01	28/12	21/12	17/08	26/08	01/02	01/03	15/02	17/09	■	22/03	08/03	12/10	19/04	07/12	26/10	09/11	11/01	07/09
Leamington	29/03	07/09	15/03	19/04	01/01	17/08	26/04	21/09	26/08	09/11	18/01	28/12	23/11	■	30/11	25/01	17/09	19/10	01/03	15/02	05/04	21/12
North Ferriby Utd.	25/01	21/09	09/11	26/08	26/04	28/12	21/12	01/01	17/08	12/10	19/04	07/09	18/01	26/10	■	15/02	07/12	29/03	05/04	01/03	15/03	17/09
Oxford City	08/02	18/01	04/01	17/09	26/08	26/04	07/09	01/03	26/12	29/03	17/08	19/04	18/03	08/03	14/12	■	28/12	05/10	09/11	30/11	19/10	26/10
Solihull Moors	21/04	15/03	12/04	05/04	26/10	05/10	08/02	19/10	01/03	14/12	30/11	25/01	24/08	11/01	14/09	20/08	■	04/01	22/03	31/08	26/12	09/11
Stalybridge Celtic	08/03	01/01	30/11	21/12	22/02	26/08	28/12	19/04	18/01	15/02	17/09	17/08	02/11	18/03	01/02	05/04	07/09	■	21/09	12/10	23/11	26/04
Stockport County	02/11	19/04	04/03	17/08	07/12	01/01	26/08	07/09	19/10	15/03	26/04	29/03	25/01	14/09	23/11	21/12	22/02	08/02	■	11/01	05/10	28/12
Vauxhall Motors	22/02	26/08	19/10	07/09	18/01	07/12	01/01	17/08	23/11	05/04	28/12	21/12	08/02	02/11	08/10	21/09	26/04	15/03	17/09	■	25/01	19/04
Worcester City	30/11	17/08	15/02	26/04	19/04	07/09	18/01	17/09	28/12	26/10	21/12	26/08	29/03	12/10	02/11	07/12	01/01	01/03	01/02	23/03	■	21/09
Workington	14/12	15/02	26/12	08/03	15/03	05/04	07/12	02/11	14/09	21/04	23/11	19/10	04/01	05/10	11/01	01/02	29/03	31/08	20/08	24/08	12/04	■

Please note that the above fixtures may be subject to change.

Football Conference South Fixtures 2013/2014 Season	Basingstoke Town	Bath City	Bishop's Stortford	Boreham Wood	Bromley	Chelmsford City	COoncord Rangers	Dorchester Town	Dover Athletic	Eastbourne Borough	Eastleigh	Ebbsfleet United	Farnborough	Gosport Borough	Havant & Waterlooville	Hayes & Yeading United	Maidenhead United	Staines Town	Sutton United	Tonbridge Angels	Weston-super-Mare	Whitehawk
Basingstoke Town	■	11/01	12/04	19/10	30/11	15/02	01/02	29/03	02/11	11/03	24/08	14/09	26/12	20/08	22/03	05/10	01/03	31/08	25/01	04/01	21/04	14/12
Bath City	22/02	■	01/02	07/12	18/01	22/03	31/08	15/03	21/09	05/04	20/08	14/12	21/04	24/08	02/11	12/04	23/11	04/01	12/10	14/09	26/12	08/02
Bishop's Stortford	21/12	17/08	■	28/12	26/08	01/01	30/11	11/03	05/04	01/03	11/01	12/10	22/03	05/10	07/09	15/02	26/04	26/10	19/04	02/11	11/02	25/01
Boreham Wood	04/02	26/10	19/08	■	05/10	05/04	26/12	11/01	25/01	15/02	31/08	22/03	04/01	14/09	30/11	24/08	12/10	21/04	09/11	01/03	14/12	12/04
Bromley	21/09	01/03	21/04	22/02	■	12/10	04/01	02/11	11/03	11/01	14/12	26/12	07/12	31/08	23/11	25/01	22/03	14/09	08/02	24/08	12/04	20/08
Chelmsford City	07/12	05/10	26/12	02/11	08/03	■	19/08	25/01	23/11	19/10	12/04	04/01	17/03	08/02	29/03	14/12	22/02	24/08	11/01	21/04	31/08	14/09
Concord Rangers	17/08	26/04	22/02	01/01	17/09	28/12	■	07/09	19/04	09/11	08/03	08/02	26/10	07/12	21/12	11/01	21/09	25/01	26/08	08/04	22/03	12/10
Dorchester Town	26/10	09/11	14/09	08/03	15/02	21/09	14/12	■	18/01	30/11	26/12	31/08	12/04	21/04	01/02	04/01	01/04	01/03	22/03	12/10	20/08	24/08
Dover Athletic	08/03	15/02	04/01	29/03	09/11	01/02	24/08	05/10	■	22/03	26/10	20/08	14/12	01/03	19/10	31/08	11/01	12/04	30/11	26/12	14/09	21/04
Eastbourne Borough	18/01	25/01	21/09	23/11	29/03	15/03	14/09	08/02	12/10	■	04/01	24/08	31/08	12/04	08/03	21/04	02/11	14/12	22/02	20/08	07/12	26/12
Eastleigh	19/04	28/12	15/03	26/04	07/09	21/12	05/10	01/01	01/01	07/12	■	25/01	01/03	18/01	26/08	29/03	08/02	19/10	17/08	23/11	01/03	05/04
Ebbsfleet United	23/11	07/09	18/01	21/09	01/01	17/09	02/11	26/04	28/12	19/04	08/10	■	01/03	19/10	17/08	08/03	26/08	15/02	21/12	29/03	01/02	07/12
Farnborough	01/01	26/08	08/02	17/09	15/03	17/08	29/03	21/12	07/09	26/04	22/02	30/11	■	23/11	28/12	12/10	19/04	11/01	08/03	25/01	02/11	05/10
Gosport Borough	28/12	19/04	29/03	15/03	26/04	26/10	05/04	26/08	17/08	21/12	12/10	22/02	01/02	■	01/01	30/11	07/09	09/11	08/10	21/09	15/02	11/01
Havant & Waterloo.	12/10	25/03	14/12	08/02	05/04	09/11	12/04	07/12	22/02	26/10	21/04	11/01	19/08	26/12	■	14/09	25/01	15/03	21/09	31/08	24/08	04/01
Hayes & Yeading Utd	08/02	21/12	19/10	19/04	17/08	07/09	15/03	05/04	26/04	26/08	21/09	26/10	18/01	22/03	01/03	■	28/12	28/01	01/01	07/12	23/11	09/11
Maidenhead United	09/11	08/03	31/08	18/01	26/10	30/11	15/02	19/10	15/03	01/02	14/09	21/04	24/08	14/12	05/10	20/08	■	26/12	05/04	12/04	04/01	29/03
Staines Town	26/04	17/09	07/12	26/08	01/02	19/04	23/11	17/08	21/12	07/09	22/03	05/04	21/09	08/03	18/01	02/11	01/01	■	28/12	08/02	12/10	22/02
Sutton United	15/03	29/03	24/08	01/02	19/10	01/03	21/04	23/11	17/09	05/10	02/11	12/04	14/09	04/01	15/02	26/12	07/12	20/08	■	14/12	18/01	31/08
Tonbridge Angels	05/04	30/11	08/03	17/08	19/04	26/08	18/01	22/02	01/01	28/12	15/02	09/11	19/10	25/03	26/04	01/02	21/12	05/10	07/09	■	15/03	26/10
Weston-super-Mare	26/08	01/01	09/11	07/09	21/12	26/04	19/10	28/12	08/02	17/08	30/11	05/10	05/04	25/01	19/04	22/02	17/09	29/03	26/10	11/01	■	08/03
Whitehawk	07/09	19/10	23/11	21/12	28/12	18/01	01/03	19/04	26/08	01/01	01/02	15/03	15/02	02/11	17/09	01/04	17/08	30/11	26/04	22/03	21/09	■

Please note that the above fixtures may be subject to change.

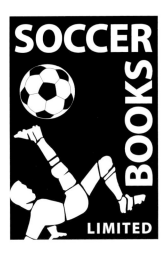

SOCCER BOOKS LIMITED

72 ST. PETERS AVENUE (Dept. SBL)
CLEETHORPES
N.E. LINCOLNSHIRE
DN35 8HU
ENGLAND

Tel. 01472 696226   Fax 01472 698546

Web site   www.soccer-books.co.uk
e-mail   info@soccer-books.co.uk

Established in 1982, Soccer Books Limited has one of the largest ranges of English-Language soccer books available. We continue to expand our stocks even further to include many more titles including German, French, Spanish and Italian-language books.

With well over 200,000 satisfied customers over the past 30 years, we supply books to virtually every country in the world but have maintained the friendliness and accessibility associated with a small family-run business. The range of titles we sell includes:

YEARBOOKS – All major yearbooks including many editions of the Sky Sports Football Yearbook (previously Rothmans), Supporters' Guides, Playfair Annuals, South and North & Central American Yearbooks, Non-League Club Directories, Almanack of World Football.

CLUB HISTORIES – Complete Statistical Records, Official Histories, Definitive Histories plus many more including photographic books.

WORLD FOOTBALL – World Cup books, European Championships History, Statistical histories for the World Cup, European Championships, South American and European Club Cup competitions and foreign-language Season Preview Magazines for dozens of countries.

BIOGRAPHIES & WHO'S WHOS – of Managers and Players plus Who's Whos etc.

ENCYCLOPEDIAS & GENERAL TITLES – Books on Stadia, Hooligan and Sociological studies, Histories and hundreds of others, including the weird and wonderful!

DVDS – Season reviews for British clubs, histories, European Cup competition finals, World Cup matches and series reviews, player profiles and a selection of almost 60 F.A. Cup Finals with many more titles becoming available all the time.

For a current printed listing of a selection of our titles, please contact us using the information at the top of this page.

Alternatively our web site offers a secure ordering system for credit and debit card holders and Paypal users and lists our full range of around 2,000 new books and over 400 DVDs.

The Supporters' Guides Series

This top-selling series has been published since 1982 and the new 2014 editions contain the 2012/2013 Season's results and tables, Directions, Photographs, Telephone numbers, Parking information, Admission details, Disabled information and much more.

THE SUPPORTERS' GUIDE TO PREMIER & FOOTBALL LEAGUE CLUBS 2014

This 30th edition covers all 92 Premiership and Football League clubs. **Price £7.99**

NON-LEAGUE SUPPORTERS' GUIDE AND YEARBOOK 2014

This 22nd edition covers all 68 clubs in Step 1 & Step 2 of Non-League football – the Football Conference National, Conference North and Conference South. **Price £7.99**

SCOTTISH FOOTBALL SUPPORTERS' GUIDE AND YEARBOOK 2014

The 21st edition featuring all Scottish Professional Football League and Highland League clubs. **Price £7.99**

THE SUPPORTERS' GUIDE TO WELSH FOOTBALL 2014

The 13th edition covers the 112+ clubs which make up the top 3 tiers of Welsh Football. **Price £7.99**

RYMAN FOOTBALL LEAGUE SUPPORTERS' GUIDE AND YEARBOOK 2012

The 2nd edition features the 66 clubs which made up the 3 divisions of the Isthmian League during the 2011/12 season. **Price £6.99**

EVO-STIK SOUTHERN FOOTBALL LEAGUE SUPPORTERS' GUIDE AND YEARBOOK 2012

This 2nd edition features the 66 clubs which made up the 3 divisions of the Southern League during the 2011/12 season. **Price £6.99**

These books are available UK & Surface post free from –

Soccer Books Limited (Dept. SBL)
72 St. Peter's Avenue
Cleethorpes, DN35 8HU
United Kingdom